GOODBYE, *LIBERTY BELLE*

GOODBYE, *LIBERTY BELLE*
A Son's Search for His Father's War

J. I. Merritt

Foreword by Samuel Hynes

First Cooper Square Press edition 2002

This Cooper Square Press hardcover edition of *Goodbye, Liberty Belle* is an unabridged, but completely redesigned republication of the edition first published in Dayton, Ohio, in 1993. It is reprinted by arrangement with the author.

Copyright © 1993 by Wright State University Press
New preface and introduction copyright © 2002 by J. I. Merritt

Excerpt from "Losses" by Randall Jarrell printed with permission from Farrar, Strauss & Giroux.

Composition and design: Barbara Werden Design

Published by Cooper Square Press
A Member of the Rowman & Littlefield Publishing Group
200 Park Avenue South, Suite 1109
New York, New York 10003-1503
www.coopersquarepress.com

Distributed by National Book Network

A previous edition of this book was catalogued as follows by the Library of Congress:

Merritt, J. I., 1944–
    Goodbye, Liberty Belle : a son's search for his father's war / J. I. Merritt
       p. cm.
    Includes bibliographical references and index.
    1. World War, 1939–1945—Aerial operations, American. 2. World War, 1939–1945—Underground movements—Yugoslavia. 3. Escapes—Yugoslavia—History—20th century. 4. Merritt, Jim. 5. Yugoslavia—Description and travel—1971– I. Title.

D790.M464 1993
940.54'4973—dc20
                                                                    92–42784 CIP

ISBN 0-8154-1231-2

FOR MY MOTHER AND FATHER

The thirties and forties are a crucial time. In young adulthood, a man may be able to drive through life assuming that things are "worked out" with father and that "my father is who he is, it doesn't matter to me," but as we are into our thirties and forties the need for reconnecting becomes more pressing.
—SAMUEL OSHERSON, *Finding Our Fathers*

In bombers named for girls we burned
The cities we had learned about in school . . .
—from "Losses," by RANDALL JARRELL

CONTENTS

FOREWORD

Goodbye, Liberty Belle is different from any other war story I have read. That is because it is really three stories. One of these is the story of Jim Merritt, Senior, a B-24 pilot in the Second World War flying out of Italy with the Fifteenth Air Force, and of his last combat flight. It's a good war story: how his plane, the *Liberty Belle*, was hit by antiaircraft fire over Vienna, how Merritt got it back over Partisan-controlled Yugoslavia before the crew bailed out, and how the Partisans got them out, in spite of rain and cold and fascist patrols. And it's a story from a theater of war that has never gotten its share of attention (because the Eighth Air Force, flying from England, got it all).

A second story is about that pilot's son, Jim Junior, who decided that he wanted to know the story of that last flight—the whole story—and who wrote letters, made phone calls, and traveled across the United States to interview survivors, get the facts, and put them together. His hunt for the story has a particular pull for a writer like myself, and I'm impressed by the author's industry and skill; but I think his account will interest anyone who has ever wanted to know what happened back then, when fathers and grandfathers were young, and has wondered how to go about finding out.

The third story—and it's as engaging as the others—tells how the two Jims, father and son, returned to Yugoslavia in 1986 to revisit the scene of the *Liberty Belle*'s crash and to meet the people who had helped the crew to escape and to reach the Adriatic—and safety.

Merritt weaves these three stories together, cutting and shifting as skillfully as a novelist, setting past against present, event against memory, using both official documents and recollections to fill out his telling. In the process he creates a lively cast of characters: crew members, both as they were in 1944 and in their older versions of the 1980s, and Yugoslavians—village elders, widows, mayors, Partisans, all done in sharp detail.

These are three stories, but they interweave into one— the story of how a son set out to discover his father by re-creating a crucial event of his father's young manhood. The two characters in this story—the eager son and the reserved, self-controlled father—are made vividly and movingly real as they struggle with language difficulties, weather, and too many toasts of *rakija*, the local brandy, until at last Jim Senior unbends and drinks a toast to "the only country to tell both Hitler and Stalin to go to hell." It's a great moment.

There is a special interest in this book now, as Yugoslavia goes through another destructive and divisive war, with much the same divisions drawn—Serbs against Croats, East against West. Merritt's book reminds us that these divisions are not abstractions, but are made of human individuals— fierce and enduring people, who are capable of both great heroism and great generosity. In that sense *Goodbye, Liberty Belle* is history, of a valuable, human kind.

Samuel Hynes
*Woodrow Wilson Professor of
Literature, Emeritus
Princeton University
Princeton, New Jersey
March 1992*

PREFACE TO THE NEW EDITION

Most of the "present" of this book is September 1986. At that time, when my father and I visited Yugoslavia, I saw little indication that the political bonds forged by Marshal Tito during and after World War II would soon dissolve, the victim of the Balkans' ancient ethnic hatreds. In the spring of 1989, when I completed the first draft of my manuscript, that union still seemed fairly secure, despite the burgeoning independence of the former Eastern Bloc states.

During our visit in 1986, the only person we met who seemed to be carrying any ethnic grudge was a Croatian-American staying at our hotel in Zagreb. His name was John. He had immigrated to the United States as a boy around 1940 and later, as an entrepreneur in the Midwestern Rust Belt, had prospered in the tool-and-die business. John had since sold his firm and moved to Florida. He was an outgoing bear of a man who instantly befriended us—taking us to dinner with the hotel manager, pulling strings with Pan American when we needed to change our plane reservations, and driving us to the airport, where he embraced us in a hearty good-bye as though we'd been intimates for years. He had the energy and subtlety of a blast furnace and spoke in a torrent of billingsgate directed at the

Serbian Communists who dominated the central government of Yugoslavia. (Our translator, Janez Zerovc, said he
was equally profane when addressing the same subject in
Serbo-Croatian.) John refused to call his native tongue anything other than "Croatian." And, counter to accepted history, he insisted that Tito wasn't a Croat but a Russian—the
implication being that no true Croat would ever have yoked
his country into a political union with Serbia, its ancient
enemy.

By early 1991, when Wright State University Press
accepted my book for publication, Yugoslavia was rent by
civil strife and on the verge of breaking apart. Indeed, a few
months later, the republics of Slovenia and Croatia seceded
from the union. The Serbians then invaded neighboring
Croatia to secure areas of the country inhabited by Serbian
minorities. As I was readying the manuscript for publication
in early 1992, thousands had already died in the war
between Croats and Serbs, and the conflict continued,
despite fourteen short-lived truces negotiated by the European Community. Obviously, our friend John knew something I had not.

The description in this book of Yugoslavia in 1986
depicts a united country that had put to rest its bloody past.
However naive this view may now seem in retrospect, I
resisted altering the text—to show, for example, some pre-
science on my part that did not exist. I should add that my
dad was less convinced than I of the durability of Tito's
state. Forty-two years before, he had seen firsthand Yugoslavians killing each other.

■

The Cooper Square Press edition of *Goodbye, Liberty Belle* is substantially the same as the one published by Wright State University Press in 1993. I corrected some typos and errors of facts, added some new information that came my way after publication of the first edition, and here and there fiddled with phrasing in the compulsive way of most authors.

Many people assisted or supported me in various ways in the research and writing of *Goodbye, Liberty Belle.* I owe a debt to Edi Selhaus and Janez Zerovc. In addition to making possible my trip to Yugoslavia, Edi's own book on the rescue by Partisans of Allied airmen, *Zbogom, Liberty Bell*, provided the inspiration for my title. I am also indebted to Ivan Dezelic of Pan American Airways, Zlatko Novak and Franjo Jagetic of the Hotel InterContinental in Zagreb, and Slovenian Americans John Rucigay and John Hribar. I thank Harry R. Fletchner and Major Lester A. Sliter of the U.S.A.F. Historical Research Center and Richard L. Boylan of the National Archives for their assistance in tracking down documentary materials. Also (for the Cooper Square Press edition) George Watson, of Lakewood, New Jersey, a former Tuskegee Airman who helped me locate Shelby Westbrook and Robert C. Chandler, the two P-51 pilots of the all-black 332nd Fighter Group who were on the ground with my father and his crew.

I am grateful to Chuck Creesy, editor of the *Princeton Alumni Weekly,* in which a portion of this story originally appeared; my friend Ann Waldron for her advice and encouragement; Anne Matthews and Peter Burford, respectively, for helping me find *Goodbye, Liberty Belle*'s first and second publishers; Carl Becker of Wright State University Press and Michael Dorr of Cooper Square Press.

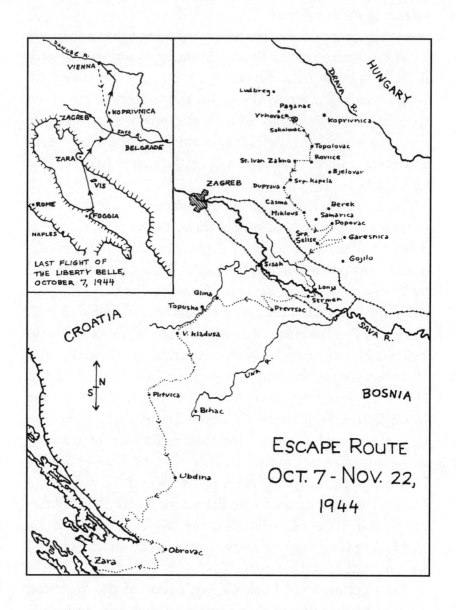

DANUBE R.
VIENNA
KOPRIVNICA
ZAGREB
SAVA R.
ZARA
BELGRADE
VIS
ROME
FOGGIA
NAPLES

LAST FLIGHT OF
THE LIBERTY BELLE,
OCTOBER 7, 1944

HUNGARY
DRAVA R.
Ludbreg
Paganac
Vrhovac
Koprivnica
Sokolovac
Topolovac
St. Ivan Zabno
Roviice
Bjelovar
ZAGREB
Duprava
Srp. kapela
Casma
Berek
Miklous
Samarica
Popovac
Srp.
Selise
Garesnica
Gojilo
Sisak
Lonja
Stermen
Glina
Topusko
Prevrsac
SAVA R.
CROATIA
V. kladusa
UNA R.
BOSNIA
S ↕ N
Plitvica
Brhac
ESCAPE ROUTE
OCT. 7 - NOV. 22,
1944
Ubdina
Obrovac
Zara

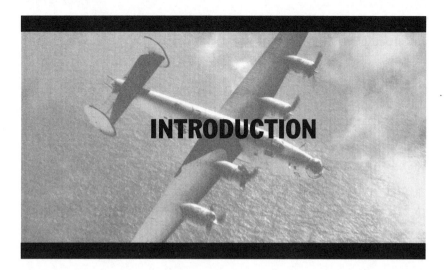

INTRODUCTION

On a flawless day in early October of 1987, my father took me flying. We had made arrangements the evening before to meet at the Mercer County Airport, a few miles from my home in central New Jersey. Dad was flying in from northern New Jersey and expected to arrive at the airport at 1:30 in the afternoon. Because (unlike me) he is punctual to a fault and had told me that he was on a tight schedule—he would be flying a rented plane and had to return it by 4:30—I made sure to get there comfortably in advance of our appointed rendezvous.

The civil-aviation terminal was nearly empty when I arrived with some minutes to spare. Seeing that Dad wasn't there, I went out onto the tarmac to wait for him.

Dad had taken up flying the previous fall, following a long hiatus. During World War II, he had been a bomber pilot and a flight instructor and later had flown for a few years in the postwar reserves. Although he loved flying and took to it as naturally as walking or sleeping, the demands of work and family had caused him to set it aside until his semi-retirement, at the age of sixty-five. The seat-of-the-pants feel for piloting a plane had never left him, and it had taken him only a few lessons to brush up his skills and become acquainted with modern instrument navigation and communications.

Waiting for him now, I recalled the excitement in his voice the previous spring, when he had called to tell me that his flight instructor had okayed him for soloing, and that for the first time in thirty-five years he had taken up a plane alone. When I said that I'd like to go up with him, he demurred until he had more flying time under his belt. Later, we made tentative arrangements for a date in September but had to scrub it because of bad weather. Today's plans represented our second attempt to fly together.

One-thirty came and went, and I was becoming just a little apprehensive when I heard a distant droning. Squinting against the glare of the cloudless sky, I watched the diminutive Piper Cherokee circle the field and come in for a landing. As it taxied up to the line of parked planes about a hundred yards away, I started walking toward it, on the hopeful assumption that it was Dad at the controls. The engine cut off, and the prop fluttered to a stop; the door opened, and a lean figure in blue slacks, a V-necked sweater, and sunglasses climbed out.

"Sorry I'm late," he said. "It took me a little longer than I expected to fill out my flight plan and get out of the Somerset airport."

It had been several months since I'd seen him. He looked his usual fit self—six-foot-two and 170 pounds (a shade shorter and lighter than myself), with iron-gray temples and a full head of dark hair framing a tanned and ruddy face.

I followed him around the low-winged plane as he made a brief preflight inspection. He opened the cowling to show me the engine, which appeared barely adequate to drive a lawn mower. The aircraft rocked easily when he pressed down on the end of one wing. After checking the movement of the tail surfaces, he uncapped the wing tank and peered in. "Fuel's okay," he said. Patting the fuselage, he added, "It's not a bad little airplane. Are you ready?"

"Let's go," I said.

We squeezed into the cramped cockpit, seated side by side, our arms nearly touching. The sun had warmed the interior like the inside of a car on a summer day, and I wrestled off my jacket and stowed it behind the passenger seat, along with my camera. The plane had dual controls, and the wheel on my side was practically against my chest. My knees nudged the instrument panel. I locked my feet to the flight deck, careful not to place them on the rudder pedals, and buckled and cinched my seat belt.

Dad switched on the ignition; the prop turned over, and the engine sputtered and caught. He idled back and radioed the tower for permission to take off. We taxied onto the runway, and after clearance from the tower, Dad shoved forward the throttle.

The little plane seemed to leap into the air. The radio crackled as we climbed and banked. We swung north, skirting the edge of my home town of Pennington—I saw the steeple of our church and the water tower at the head of our street; I tried to spot our house, but it was obscured by trees—and headed out over the rolling countryside of western New Jersey. In the distance I could see, nestled in the low green hills, Spruce Run and Round Valley reservoirs, the ribbon of Interstate 78 and, hazy on the horizon, the Delaware Water Gap and Pocono Plateau.

Beyond Route 78, at my request, we dropped down to a thousand feet to swing over the part of the Musconetcong

River where I fish for trout. The Musky cut through a patch-work of green and brown farm fields, and through a fringe of trees the sun glanced off the stream's familiar runs and riffles. Dad banked the plane steeply while I snapped photographs. After a second pass, we climbed again to our cruising altitude of 2,100 feet and got back on our flight path.

"Do you want to fly it?" he asked.

It was not a question I had expected. "Sure," I said, although I was happy simply watching the scenery.

I had never flown an airplane, and I quickly discovered how hard it can be. Unlike driving a car, you have to control your direction in three dimensions rather than two. You're not anchored to a road but adrift in a liquid medium. The plane slips and slides on the wind and behaves with a mind of its own. I struggled with the controls, trying to dampen the swings of the floating magnetic compass while simultaneously holding altitude. I found that I could maintain heading or altitude but not both at once. I worried that, by overcorrecting for our dropping altitude, I might bring the nose too high and stall, sending the plane into a spin. Dad didn't say anything. I had expected that he would let me fly for a few minutes just to get a feel for it, but it seemed like an eternity before he volunteered to take the controls again.

Heading north-northwest, we picked up U.S. 80 as it skirted the Delaware River off to our left. At the Delaware Water Gap, where the river cuts through the leading edge of the Appalachians, we turned right and followed along the Kittatinny Ridge; the sumac and maples along its flat-topped summit were just beginning to flame into their fall colors. Dad tried to explain to me the radio navigation system that made getting between points at once so much easier and more complicated than it had been during his flying days more than forty years before. As we passed the airport at Hackettstown, he pointed out a radio transmitter on the ground—it looked like a giant white shirt-stud—that broadcast one of the continuous signals used by pilots to triangulate their positions. Although I understood the concept, most of the details were lost on me. I really wasn't paying much attention anyway, being content to revel in the smoky landscape. I recalled the last time we had been in an airplane together, thirteen months before, not as pilot and passenger in a single-engine plane but aboard a Pan Am jetliner over the Atlantic, returning from Yugoslavia.

"Do you want to fly her again?" he asked, as we headed back toward Trenton.

"That's okay—thanks!"

The airport came into view. Dad got his instructions from the tower. As we approached the end of the runway, I noticed on the grass beside it a bright green light that I assumed must be some kind of directional beacon. Dad throttled back, the plane dropped, and the green light blinked off the instant before our wheel brushed the ground in a flawless three-point landing.

"Beautiful!" Dad said, and so it was. "Did you notice how that light seemed to go out just as we hit the runway? That means your approach and touch-down are perfect."

We taxied up to the parking lane, and Dad shut off the engine. As we walked to the terminal, he grinned and squeezed my shoulder.

"Congratulations," he said. "You're the first passenger I've taken up since 1945!"

Our flight had taken longer than anticipated, and he was running further behind schedule. He wanted to call the

Somerset airport to say that he'd be late returning, but I told
him that I would do it for him.

"Thanks," he said. "I better be going."

"Have a good flight," I said. "Thanks again!"

"So long, Jimbo!"

He walked briskly back to the plane. There was a bounce
to his step that belied his sixty-seven years. I waited on the
tarmac outside the terminal, waiting for him to take off. The
plane taxied to the end of the runway and was quickly airborne. I resisted for a few moments going inside to make his
telephone call and instead remained on the tarmac,
watching the plane grow smaller until it disappeared on the
horizon.

I laughed at the revelation about my being his first passenger in forty-two years. Although I could still feel the grip
of his hand on my shoulder, our flight was already settling
into memory, the mind working its subtle filtering and shifting of details. But it was another memory, from the year
before, that my mind fixed on as I entered the door of the
terminal and caught my middle-aged reflection in the glass.
We were flying home from Yugoslavia. The anxiety and
uncertainty about that trip was behind us; in their place was
a sense of relief and triumph. At that moment, we were perhaps closer than we would ever be again. Dad smiled and
tousled my hair, a gesture that dissolved years and made me
gasp. For that brief instant, I was a boy again, my father's
child.

Chapter 1
THE MISSION

He was out of the airplane in an instant. Rolling in the slipstream, he glimpsed the bomber's big twin tails flash by. Such an eerie sensation, and so different from what he expected. There was no fear, no sense of falling. He felt suspended over the gentle landscape of farm fields and green forested hills. Silence enveloped him; until this moment, he hadn't realized how chaotically noisy it had been all the time he had struggled with the dying plane, its propellers screaming out of synch on either side of the shattered cockpit. It occurred to him that, someday, he would like to fly a glider.

Pull the ripcord!

Loosed from his reverie, he reached across his chest, grasped the brass handle of the parachute ripcord, and yanked. He waited for the reassuring POP! of the spring-loaded chute and the swift rush of nylon behind him. Instead he heard—nothing.

He gave the ripcord a second jerk.

Again nothing.

Damn!

The ridge was coming up fast, and he was close enough

to see that the clearings farther down the slope were vine-yards.

He cursed again and with every ounce of strength pulled the ripcord a third time.

■

Jim Merritt (my father) was twenty-four years old and the pilot of a B-24 Liberator bomber when he flew his last mission over Nazi-occupied Europe. The raid on Vienna that day—October 7, 1944—had been designated a "maximum effort" by the Fifteenth Air Force, and in a few more hours nearly four hundred heavy bombers would be droning north from Italy to strike at the oil depots and refineries of the Austrian capital.

The Fifteenth Air Force had been operating out of southern Italy since the previous winter. It had moved there from bases in North Africa following the Allied invasion at Salerno and the German retreat north, occupying a score of abandoned Luftwaffe airfields amid the olive groves and sculpted hills of the Italian boot. Accommodations were spartan. San Giovanni, where Merritt and his crew had been stationed since arriving overseas in mid-September as a replacement unit assigned to the 455th Bomb Group, was typical, a flotilla of G.I. tents swimming in mud during the rainy season and baking under the relentless Italian sun during the dry. Each of the 455th's four squadrons boasted its own tent city, subdivided into separate neighborhoods for officers and enlisted. Toilets—open-ground latrines—were a short distance away, while a farther jog over the hill stood a line of showers whose spigots miraculously spewed hot water, the base's sole luxury.

Enlisted men were assigned six to a tent, officers four. The tents were sixteen-foot square, made of canvas, and about as watertight as colanders. For extra protection against the rain, some of the men hung tarps over their cots; sometimes after a big downpour, a tarp would sag under its load of water and come crashing down on the occupant of the bunk that it was meant to protect. The floor of the tent was dirt, although for twenty dollars the local Italians would cover it with a wooden deck.

Merritt and the three other officers in his crew bunked together in the same tent—the leakiest in the squadron, they were convinced. Although they had been together only five months, in the intensity of training and combat it had seemed much longer. Bombardier Keith Martin, age twenty, was a curly-haired kid born and raised in Los Angeles, an only child away from southern California for the first time and slightly homesick. Navigator Carl Rudolph was twenty-three, a cheerful Pennsylvanian and an engineer by training, the only member of the crew besides Merritt to have completed college. Copilot Bob Smith, at age nineteen the youngest of the group, occupied the fourth bunk.

Like every morning in the three weeks since the crew's arrival at San Giovanni, this one began routinely enough, with the squadron orderlies making wake-up rounds in the predawn darkness. After stumbling into their khakis and over to the latrine, they trudged down the tent-lined street to the cluster of stone farm buildings that constituted squadron headquarters. In the mess hall, a few made the usual jokes about the acid coffee, vulcanized pancakes, and congealed mass of powdered eggs diced into single servings—"square eggs," they called them—but except for grumbling about the consistently atrocious food, no one said very much. Most were only half awake, and it was still too early to talk or even to think. Anyway, better to keep your mind blank than dwelling on what the day might bring.

Outside the mess hall, they loaded into trucks that took them to group headquarters for the mission briefings—the enlisted men's first, followed by the officers'. The first ones into the briefing room moved past the M.P.s guarding the door and went directly to the front row of benches. The room always filled from front to rear. Merritt was near the front, and like the others he stared with morbid curiosity at the curtain on the wall before them. Obscured behind the curtain was a map of southern Europe overlaid with an acetate sheet, with a white string pinned to the map marking the route to target. A few men speculated about the mission, attempting nervous jokes about it—a milk run, perhaps, to hit German airfields near Athens or rail bridges in northern Italy. Targets like Vienna and Munich were another matter. They lay deep in enemy territory and were guarded by cordons of antiaircraft batteries that could lay a carpet of flak, as the saying went, "thick enough to walk on." The last mission flown by the Fifteenth, on October 4, had been over Munich, and the flak had been so intense that one of the bombardiers had jumped from his plane out of sheer terror.

The crowded room smelled of sweat and shaving lotion and was thick with cigarette smoke. The rumble of conversation stopped abruptly with the entrance of the briefing officers. The men snapped to attention. "Be seated, gentlemen," said the group commander. The briefing began with the intelligence officer, a captain, pulling the curtain on the map.

Not unexpectedly, the string on the map led from San Giovanni to Vienna. Since the Munich raid three days before, the command had twice scheduled missions to Vienna, only to scrub them because of weather; it was an open secret that the Austrian capital remained the Fifteenth's immediate top priority. A chorus of groans and catcalls greeted the choice.

Ignoring the protests, the intelligence officer moved briskly through his presentation. Other briefing officers covered weather, operations, and communications. A total of sixteen bomb groups, comprising some 390 planes, would be attacking oil depots and refineries in the Vienna area. The target for the 455th and seven other groups would be the Winterhafen oil depot, a complex of storage tanks located on the outskirts of Vienna. Each plane would be carrying eight five-hundred-pound bombs—four thousand pounds in total. The route to target would be the usual zigzag to avoid concentrations of flak guns while over enemy territory. They would fly up the Adriatic to the Dalmatian coast, cut across Yugoslavia, clip the western corner of Hungary, then slant northwest for the last leg to Vienna. A fighter escort of P-51s and P-38s from bases north of San Giovanni would rendezvous near the Yugoslav-Hungarian border an hour before target. Fighter opposition, as it had been for the last several months, would probably be light. The Germans were chronically short of fuel by this point in the war, and while they still had plenty of serviceable aircraft, they were running out of trained pilots.

As always, the biggest concern would be flak: with an estimated five hundred antiaircraft batteries, Vienna was as heavily protected as any city in the shrinking Axis realm. The crews for today's mission could count on the flak being "intense, accurate, heavy"—or simply "IAH," as noted in the mission summaries—with most of it coming from batteries armed with the German 88-millimeter cannon, one of the war's most versatile and effective weapons. Directed by radar, the 88s could throw a twenty-two-pound shell six miles high. The Germans had perfected their antiaircraft tactics, concentrating the 88s in *Grossbatterien* of up to forty guns firing a barrage of shells fused to explode at the same altitude as the bombers. The batteries were manned by old men, boys, and women, a fact that lessened not a whit their deadly effectiveness. Ultimately, flak would account for more than thirty-five hundred American planes lost over Europe in 1944, nearly six hundred more than Luftwaffe fighters.

Oil depots and refineries were the Fifteenth Air Force's most strategically important targets, with more than 80 percent of German oil production located within the eight-hundred-mile radius of its heavy bombers. The Germans defended their petroleum resources fiercely. In raids on Vienna and the Rumanian refineries at Ploesti, the Fifteenth averaged heavier losses than those suffered by the rival Eighth Air Force against manufacturing targets in northern Germany. The Eighth was more than twice as big as the Fifteenth Air Force and based in England rather than in remote southern Italy; as a result, it got the lion's share of publicity. Adding insult to injury, the Eighth Air Force enjoyed London for a watering hole instead of squalid Naples, while its airmen lived in real buildings (even if they were just metal-roofed huts) rather than tents. In the converted stables that passed for officer and N.C.O. clubs at the Fifteenth's Italian bases, the men sang a rueful parody of the famous Bogart-Bergman love theme: *It's still the same old story, the Eighth gets all the glory, while we go out to die . . . the fundamental things apply, as flak goes by.*

The briefing ended with a short pep talk from the wing commander, who emphasized the importance of the mission and wished them luck—well-meaning words that made no one feel better. The group commander led them in the ritual of synchronizing watches. Like everyone else in the room, Merritt followed the second hand on his watch. When the hand arrived at twelve, he pulled the winding knob, stopping the movement. "Gentlemen, in ten seconds it will be zero seven forty," the C.O. announced. "Ten, nine, eight, seven . . . *Hack!*" After setting his watch on the announced time, Merritt waited for the end of the countdown, then snapped the knob in place; the watch began ticking exactly on 7:40. Dismissed, they filed out to pick up their "flimsies," orders typed on onion-skin paper detailing the mission's route, schedule, and radio call names.

Waiting trucks took the crews to their planes. As they rumbled toward the bombers parked at the far end of the field, Merritt's mind drifted from the details of the briefing. He had been in Italy for less than a month and had flown his first mission less than three weeks ago. While this was only his fifth mission, he had taken combat flying in stride and was beginning to feel like a veteran. His previous targets had been factories at Bratislava, Czechoslovakia; railroad bridges on the Po River in northern Italy; air bases near Athens; and railroad marshaling yards at Munich. At that point in the war, fifty missions earned an airman a ticket home. Because Munich, Vienna, and certain other targets deemed especially hazardous counted double, Merritt would have eight missions to his credit after today's. Scuttlebutt said that the odds of completing a tour were about fifty-fifty, and he was convinced he would be in the half that made it—a positive attitude bolstered by the assumption, however spurious, that getting blown out of the sky was something that happened to the other guy.

From the beginning of his military career he had wanted to be a pilot. As an ROTC cadet at Princeton he was assigned to the field artillery, but at the earliest opportunity he had applied for transfer to the Air Corps and flight training, only to be turned down for near-sightedness and high blood pressure. So, after receiving his commission in June 1942, he opted for the tank destroyers, duty that at least promised to get him overseas to fight Rommel's panzers in North Africa. For advanced training the Army sent him to Camp Hood, Texas, a place he enjoyed despite the heat and rattlesnakes—it was exciting going out on field maneuvers, blowing up targets with bazookas and other exotic weapons. Like a lot of young men fresh out of college and with no attachments, he was having the time of his life. Any connection between the pyrotechnics of training and real combat—where the enemy shot back and you might actually get killed—was little more than an afterthought.

Soon enough, life became more complicated. A former college friend fixed him up with a blind date, a brunette divorcée with a four-year-old daughter and the improbably southern name of Jonnie Francis. Just four months later, on June 6, 1943, they were married, and at age twenty-three he found himself at once both a husband and a father. They married on short notice, with only her widowed mother and younger sister in attendance. His mother and father lived two thousand miles away, on Long Island, and would not meet their new daughter-in-law until the following fall, when they made the long train ride out to Texas; by then, she was several months pregnant and miserable with morning sickness.

At Camp Hood, meanwhile, he retook, and this time passed, the Air Corps physical; miraculously, his eyes had reverted to twenty-twenty, and his hypertension was under control. His battalion commander, a wiry lieutenant colonel who just weeks before had pushed through his promotion to first lieutenant, shook his head in disgust as he signed the transfer orders. "You disappoint me, Merritt," he grumbled. "You're a good soldier with a great future in the tank destroyers. Now you're going over to that damned sloppy Air Corps. You'll probably wind up like every other fly boy I've ever seen, walking around with the grommet out of his hat."

The colonel was referring to the ring of spring steel inside a peaked hat which kept it properly flared. An airman removed the grommet so it didn't get in the way of the earphones he wore when flying. That, at least, was the ostensibly practical reason. Of course, the floppy look also conveyed a certain panache that went with the romance of flying.

Following a ten-day honeymoon in Galveston, and with grommet still firmly in place, he started primary flight school at Cuero Field, Texas. It was a pleasant three months of nine-to-five duty that allowed him to come home each evening to their first residence, the rented first floor of a farmhouse a few miles from the base. Basic and advanced training followed at Waco and Brooks Fields, respectively. It was during the seven months of transition school at Tarrant Field, where he learned to fly B-24s, that their son was born.

They were living in a motel in nearby Fort Worth. Returning to Tarrant after a long training flight one April night, he found the field socked in by clouds and the control tower rerouting all planes to a field in Oklahoma. The baby was due any day, and something told him to get home, whatever it took. His instruments indicated that the field was almost directly below. He looked for an opening in the clouds. Finding none, he pressed the radio call button and reported to the tower.

"There's a big break in the overcast right below me. Request permission to land."

He was already descending when the tower came back with an affirmative. Plunging through the thick gray soup, he broke out over the field at five hundred feet and touched down on the runway; in the entire group, his was the only plane to make it into Tarrant that night.

His hunch proved right. Back at the motel, Jonnie Frances had started labor. The next morning he drove her to the Waco hospital. The attending obstetrician, who arrived off the golf course smelling of whiskey, hardly inspired confidence. Compounding the expectant father's anxiety was the long and difficult labor, which went on through the day and into the next night. His son turned out to be a breach baby who balked at entering the world, and when delivery finally came shortly after sunrise on April 23, it seemed a miracle.

Mother and son were still recuperating a week later when he said good-bye to them, perhaps for good. His orders were to Fresno, California, and assignment to pick up a crew for combat training. On completion of training he expected to be shipped overseas immediately, with little chance for furlough. At Fresno they sent him down to March Field, east of Los Angeles, where the duty officer gave him some welcome and completely unexpected news: A new class of B-24 crews had just started training, and another class wouldn't begin for two weeks. Until then, the officer advised, "You might as well go home."

He hopped a military cargo plane and within twelve hours was back in Waco, arriving unannounced for a joyous reunion. Several days later, the young lieutenant and his wife left their two kids with his mother-in-law and drove their 1940 Plymouth across southern New Mexico and Arizona to Riverside, California, where they lived in a rented room while he went through training with his new combat crew. The intense ten weeks of training included hundreds of hours of night flying over the ocean and desert; their time together was sporadic, and more often than not she slept alone. On a rare free weekend they went up to Lake Arrowhead with another officer and his pregnant wife. To impress them with his nautical skills gained from boyhood summers on Long Island, he took all of them sailing and capsized the boat, scaring the wits out of the expectant parents.

He and his crew completed training in August. The colonel who addressed them at graduation praised the class as the best that had ever passed through March Field. Merritt had been in the service long enough not to take such pronouncements seriously; nonetheless, he took pride in the performance of his men, who in the course of training garnered honors as crew of the week, with their picture featured on the front page of the base newspaper, the March Field *Beacon*.

The next stop would be Hamilton Field, near San Francisco, and assignment overseas. It was time to say goodbye again. When he boarded the train at the Riverside station, Jonnie Frances was the only wife present who wasn't dissolved in tears. "I'm just not like that," she would say later. Whatever happened now, they had had this time together. Despite the long, unpredictable hours of training and the night flying, their ten weeks in Riverside had been a reprieve. The memory of it sustained him on the cross-country troop train and the transatlantic passage to war.

■

When Merritt arrived at the Liberator assigned to him, the enlisted members of the crew were already there and had begun picking through the flight clothes and other gear piled next to the bomber. The Libs were unpressurized and as drafty as barns, and the demands of flying them in combat at twenty-three thousand feet or more, where the temperature was a bone-numbing minus-fifty degrees, made for a forbidding wardrobe. Most of the men fought the cold with electrically heated "monkey suits." These plugged into outlets and could be subject to failure, sometimes shorting out if the occupant happened to sweat too much. (Easy enough when running a gauntlet of flak while in a plane loaded with two tons of explosives.) A few preferred the bulky but dependable leather and fleece-lined flight suits. Additional items included gloves, oxygen mask, insulated boots, leather flight helmet, goggles, and a 45-caliber service automatic carried in a shoulder holster. A yellow "Mae West" inflatable life jacket slipped over the neck and was secured with straps under the crotch and around the waist. Parachutes came in three varieties: seat pack, chest pack, and back pack. A seat pack made a nice cushion and came in handy as a flak-stopper, but it was bulkier than a chest pack, which could be unsnapped from its harness and stowed until needed. Each man also carried an "escape kit" for use if they went down in enemy territory. The kits held medicine, morphine, vitamin pills, water purification tablets, chocolate, fifty dollars in U.S. currency, a small brass compass, a language phrase guide, and silk maps of Europe.

Finally—carried on board and donned as they approached the target—were steel helmet and canvas flak vest lined with steel plates. The sum total of clothing and accouterments came to some sixty pounds. An airman in full battle regalia waddled to his station, as mobile as a four-year-old smothered in a snowsuit.

Two of the regular crew members, copilot Bob Smith and waist gunner Len Cole, were grounded with head colds, and substitutes had been assigned to their positions. A southern Californian named Don Maes would be flying as copilot. He was of medium height, with a round face, blond hair, and an incipient overseas moustache. Merritt had met him for the first time several days before but knew little about him, except that he had been in Italy a month longer and had flown about a dozen more missions.

Maes was twenty-two years old and had left behind a young wife who was now five months pregnant with their first child. He and Arline had gone together during high school near Los Angeles and the two years following graduation, when he attended junior college and worked in a defense plant. They were married a few months before his enlistment in the Air Corps, in September 1942. Their lives were typical of service couples flung about by the whims of war. After earning his commission and completing pilot training, he was assigned to twin-engine school and then to Waco as a flight instructor. Against all probability, he hoped to finish out the war there. He was in the air one morning

with a student pilot when the tower called and ordered him
back to base. Waiting for him were orders for B-24 transition school in Nevada.

He arrived in Italy six months later, ferrying a brand-new
Liberator from Hamilton Field via Newfoundland, the
Azores, and Tunisia. Landing at Bari, he was discomfited to
see, spread out before him, a boneyard of flak-shredded B-
24s being cannibalized for parts. Later, he wondered if they
had been put there to give virgin crews an inkling of things
to come.

By now, Maes had flown twenty missions and was nearly
halfway through his tour. (When he started, an airman
could return to the States after thirty-five missions, but
recently the magic number had been upped to fifty.) He
expected to be made a first pilot soon, with his own crew to
command, but for now he reconciled himself to flying at
least the next mission with nine men he scarcely knew. There
was a frightful arbitrariness to assignment as a substitute
crewman, given the certainty that, on any mission, some
percentage of planes weren't going to make it back. He took
slight comfort in knowing that Arline was at home with her
family, and that his brother-in-law had a letter from him and
instructions to give it to her if he failed to return from a mission. Pending confirmation of death or capture, he assured
her, anyone who did not get back was routinely reported
missing in action. Many crews, he added, were bailing out
over Yugoslavia and escaping to Italy with help from
antifascist guerrillas.

The other substitute was a lanky staff sergeant from
Sterling, Colorado, named Art Johnson. Twenty-one years
old and a veteran of thirty missions (including two over

Vienna), he had started out in one of the 455th's sixteen original crews that had arrived in Italy the previous January. His crew enjoyed phenomenal luck, surviving its thirty-five missions without a scratch—the only one of the sixteen to do so. In June the crew cycled home, but Johnson stayed behind. With five missions to go his sinus tubes had collapsed, landing him in a Naples hospital for several weeks. Returning to group headquarters, he remained grounded pending a full recovery and a return to flight duty to complete his tour. For the next three months he served as group clerk, a job whose duties included filling out missing-in-action reports for crews that failed to return from their missions.

Among the headquarters staff, Johnson was known for his calm dependability and maturity, qualities not always present in a population whose median age was that of a first-semester college junior. His mother, a devout Methodist, prayed for him and his brother, an infantryman fighting his way up the Italian peninsula, and never doubted they would come home safely. Prior to enlisting, he had attended college for a year and a half and had become engaged to a girl named Polly, but they had postponed their marriage after his crew received orders to ship overseas on short notice.

The doctors had recently declared Johnson fit for flying. Today's mission would be the first he had flown since being grounded the previous May. He was glad to be going, for the sooner he began racking up sorties again, the quicker he would complete his tour and rotate home. Although his faith told him he would make it, it seemed prudent to hedge his bets; he left his diaries with a college buddy on headquarters staff, with instructions to deliver them to his fiancée if he didn't return.

The men busied themselves putting on their gear and running through the preflight routine. Gunners checked their guns and ammunition while the armorer made sure the bombs were properly secured in the bombbay racks. The flight engineer climbed up on the wings to eyeball fuel levels in each of the plane's four tanks. One by one they entered the plane—stooping down and swinging under the open bombbay doors, hoisting themselves up onto the narrow catwalk, then crawling either forward or aft between the menacing five-hundred-pounders.

Merritt went aboard last. Before doing so, he walked around the plane, checking tires, landing gear, tail-skid, and control surfaces; all looked okay. The plane was a B-24H, a relatively new model of the Liberator. Its aluminum skin gleamed in the morning sun; unlike older Libs in the Fifteenth, it had been spared the traditional coat of olive-drab camouflage, which added several hundred pounds of weight to an already overburdened plane. Its tall, twin tails bore the markings of the 455th Bomb Group—a black diamond floating above a yellow field— and serial number 250425. Like virtually every heavy bomber in a combat theater, this one sported a moniker: emblazoned on its nose was a scantily clad female and the name *Liberty Belle*.

The *Liberty Belle* had been built by the Consolidated company the year before at a plant in Fort Worth, Texas, for a cost of $300,000 and had joined the Fifteenth Air Force in early 1944. It was one of more than eighteen thousand B-24s built during the war—about five thousand more than the better known B-17 Flying Fortress, with which it was usually compared unfavorably. On paper anyway, the B-24 was the better airplane. In its earlier configurations it could fly higher, faster, and farther than a Fortress with the same bomb load, although modifications to improve its firepower against enemy fighters (particularly the addition of a nose turret) played havoc with its aerodynamics. In the view of most pilots familiar with both aircraft, the B-24 was the more difficult to fly. Many, too, believed that the Fortress could take more punishment and keep on flying; others regarded this as propaganda dispensed by the Eighth Air Force, which consisted overwhelmingly of B-17s.

There was also the matter of esthetics. The Fortress's cigar-shaped fuselage and sloping tail gave it a grace lacking in the B-24. Detractors of the Liberator dubbed it the "flying boxcar" and "the crate the B-17 came in." Others—Merritt included—claimed to like its lines, at least in the air, when its sleek Davis wing could be seen to better advantage.

On the ground, however, even its defenders conceded that the Lib was ugly. Like all B-24s, the *Liberty Belle* with its boxy, low-slung fuselage looked about as gainly as a barnyard goose. Merritt wondered how they ever got off the ground with their overload of fuel, bombs, and men. For long missions like today's a plane might carry several tons more than the manufacturer's "red-line" gross weight of sixty-five thousand pounds, a third of it bombs and fuel. Compounding the liftoff problem were the Fifteenth's short runways, built originally for German fighters. A bomber pilot needed every inch of the mile-long strips, bouncing along in the prop-wash of the plane in front of him as the Liberators struggled to get airborne at twenty-five-second intervals. On some mornings not all of them made it.

Climbing up to the flight deck, Merritt settled into the

left-hand seat and with Maes began preparing for takeoff. Behind them the flight engineer, Corbo, reached overhead to open the valves controlling fuel to each engine. With ignition switches off, a ground crewman came forward to pull each of the four big propellers through by hand, clearing any oil or fuel in the combustion chambers. For the next ten minutes, pilot and copilot went through the litany of pre-flight checks, with Maes reading from a laminated card and Merritt responding to each item as it was executed.

        "Ignition switches"—"On."
        "Generator switches"—"Off."
        "Brake"—"Set."
        "Automatic flight control"—"Off."
        "De-icer controls"—"Off."
        "Cowl flaps"—"Open."
        "Superchargers"—"Off."

And so on down the check list. With the pre-ignition steps completed, they paused until a green flare from the operations building arced across the field, signaling them to start engines.

The engines—numbering one through four, left to right— were started, beginning with the inboard right (number three), which ran the generator that supplied power to the others. Four, two, and one followed in sequence, the procedure identical for each: open the throttle, hit the primer button, throw the meshing switch; prime some more as the engine cranked over and exploded into life. A cloud of blue-gray smoke enveloped the cowling and swirled away in the prop wind. The roar and vibration increased as each of the twelve-hundred-horsepower Pratt & Whitney engines turned over and fired in succession. Maes nudged the throttles forward, increasing the R.P.M. to one thousand while monitoring the temperature and the oil and manifold pressures. With all engines running and props synchronized, a ground crewman removed the wheel chocks. Merritt released the brake and with the outboard throttles and rudder pedals steered the *Liberty Belle* forward, joining the line of other Liberators taxiing toward the runway.

Twenty-eight bombers were now queued up and ready to go, trembling like hornets, spewing smoke and rending the morning air with a roar that penetrated to the bone. Waiting for takeoff, Merritt and Maes worked through the last of their preflight checkoffs. Exercise props throughout their pitch range. Adjust control tabs. Place mixture controls on auto-rich. Increase R.P.M. to two thousand and hold while checking manifold pressure and magneto switches. Set superchargers. Wing flaps down, cowl flaps open one third, generators on.

On the flagman's signal, the lead bomber lurched forward and waddled down the runway, hugging the ground as it accelerated with agonizing slowness. Its chance of becoming airborne seemed about as likely as a bowling ball's. Miraculously, as it neared the end of the runway it lifted off and tucked in its landing gear, clearing the olive groves and turning in a long arc toward the formation point. Within half a minute the next bomber followed, then the next and the next.

The *Liberty Belle* moved up the line and swung into position as soon as the bomber ahead of it started down the runway. Merritt set the brakes and pushed the throttles to the firewall, waiting for the other plane to gain a safe distance. Straining, the *Liberty Belle* hunkered down against the thrust of her engines. He released the brake, and the overloaded bomber trundled forward, gaining speed; as she bounced along the steel-mesh runway, he kept his eyes on the horizon while Maes read off their ground speed: "Sixty, seventy, eighty, ninety. . . ." They were now past the point of safely stopping and were committed to takeoff. The olive grove at the end of the runway loomed larger, the trees assuming individual shapes. "One hundred, one hundred ten, one hundred fifteen, one hundred twenty. . . ." Merritt eased back the wheel and felt thirty-two tons of airplane heave into the air, the trees slipping beneath them as Maes raised the landing gear and flaps. With the *Liberty Belle* now safely above stalling speed, he let go his breath and turned the plane toward the assembly point.

Seven planes composed a squadron, flying in a combat box, which was meant to assure a tight grouping of bombs on target while maximizing the firepower of the bombers' machine guns against enemy fighters. "Box" was something of a misnomer; from above or below, the formation looked more like a pair of linked diamonds. The lead bomber, flown by the most experienced crew, was out in front, with two other planes off its quarter and slightly lower. A second trio flew below and slightly behind the first group. The *Liberty Belle* was flying in the seventh and last slot, known as Tail-End Charlie. Later, navigator Carl Rudolph would ponder the significance of their flying in the seventh position, on the seventh day of the month, on their seventh sortie.

Assembling always seemed to take forever. The bombers wheeled in immense circles, individual planes forming into squadrons, squadrons into groups, groups into wings. A fully loaded Liberator was about as easy to fly as a Mack truck with wings, and jockeying one around the sky while playing snap-the-whip with the lead bomber could leave a pilot wringing with sweat. Flying Tail-End Charlie compounded the difficulties, and Merritt was relieved when the formations were at last in order, leaving the Italian coast behind and heading north over the Adriatic.

As the *Liberty Belle* climbed gradually to cruising altitude, her ten-man crew settled into the routine of the three-hour flight to target. Only the pilot and copilot had very much to do; the definition of war as long bouts of tedium broken by moments of terror was never more true than for bomber crews. In the plane's forwardmost position, nose gunner Artie Dupree, a lanky and engaging twenty-year-old from Laurel, Mississippi, sat back in his turret and watched the morning sun winking off the Adriatic. Directly behind him, in the navigator's space, Rudolph plotted their position every few minutes and recorded it in a log.

In the bombardier's space immediately below Rudolph, Martin made his usual preparations for combat, spreading out a pair of flak jackets on the deck and hanging two more on either side of him. These were in addition to the one he would put on as they neared the target. He also wore a seat-pack parachute whose two inches of tightly folded nylon could quite literally save his butt from flying shards of steel. For extra insurance he kept at hand a chest-pack parachute to snap on if they had to bail out; it also made a nice pillow for resting against the bulkhead.

Barely twenty, Martin was the youngest of the crew's officers. Although chafing under the discipline and conformity of military life, he was a superb bombardier. He had huge hands, but his touch on the control knobs of the Norden bombsight was as sensitive as a safecracker's. Like many bombardiers and navigators he had started out in pilot training. He had shown a knack for flying and executed an eight-point roll the first time he ever tried it. But overconfidence proved his undoing: after flipping his Stearman trainer during a landing he washed out of flight school. So he became a bombardier—potentially the best in the 455th Bomb Group, and maybe too skillful for his own good. The command wanted to send him to lead bombardier school, which would mean leaving the crew and almost certainly being assigned to a new one on his return. The thought filled him with dread. The crew had become like a surrogate family; if anything were going to happen to him, he didn't want it to be with a bunch of guys he scarcely knew.

Despite their differences in age and temperament, Merritt liked Martin and looked on him as he might a kid brother. Each respected the other for his abilities. During the crew's training in the California desert, Martin boasted of having the best pilot in the group. With little to do on most flights, he often read a newspaper or simply snoozed; Merritt's landings, he said, were so smooth that he could sleep right through them.

In Italy, Martin had objected more than most to the rigors of tent life. Carl Rudolph recalled a particular incident. Shortly after their arrival at San Giovanni, Martin had resolved to improve accommodations by jury-rigging a stove out of a fifty-gallon drum and an old oxygen tank. The drum went inside the tent. The tank hung from an olive tree next to the tent and was filled with hundred-octane fuel, which dripped through a copper tube onto rocks placed in the bottom of the drum. When the fuel burned, it heated the rocks, and the metal walls of the drum radiated warmth. The stove was hot enough to cook on and proved a smashing success until one rainy morning when Martin fired it using a rolled newspaper for a torch. To put out the flaming newspaper, he dipped it in the water-filled storm trench running the perimeter of the tent. *Poof!* Unknown to him, fuel had leaked into the trench and was now burning furiously, along with the tent itself. Someone grabbed Rudolph's expensive "Palm Beach" uniform jacket and began beating the flames with it, but the rain doused the fire before too much damage was done.

Rudolph also remembered returning from a mission with a thousand-pound bomb that failed to release over the target. When they reached the Adriatic, Merritt opened the bombbay doors and Martin crawled out on the catwalk with a screwdriver to pry the bomb loose. Noticing a fishing boat, and assuming it probably belonged to the enemy, Martin timed the bomb's release in an attempt to hit it. Fortunately, it fell well wide of the mark, splashing harmlessly into the sea.

■

On the flight deck, aft of the compartments for the bombardier and navigator, Merritt and Maes took turns in the constant struggle to keep the *Liberty Belle* locked in formation—nudging the throttles forward whenever she began slipping too far from the other planes while simultaneously pulling back on the wheel to counteract the Liberator's tendency to drop its nose when accelerating; then, as the plane mushed forward, easing back on the throttles ever so gently, resisting the temptation to overcontrol.

Two other crewmen shared the flight deck with the pilot and copilot. The engineer and top-turret gunner was Nick Corbo. Dark, slight, and serious, the third oldest in a family of eight children from upstate New York, he had celebrated

his twentieth birthday just four days earlier. Next to him, a
rail-thin electronics wiz and former ham-radio enthusiast
named Robert Wheeler manned the radio console.

In his two years of service, Wheeler had come to know
better than most about the vagaries of chance and military
bureaucracy. Enlisting straight out of high school, he had
been posted to a top-secret school in the new technology of
radar. The Army assured him that he would later be given
officer training and placed in charge of a crew of radar spe-
cialists. Instead of an officer's future, however, he was
assigned to the Air Corps and ordered to basic training at
Fresno. Any lingering hopes of convincing the Army to reas-
sign him as a radar engineer were dashed when a disgruntled
recruit burned down the administration building, destroying
all personnel files and his record of attendance at the secret
radar school.

Following basic, he was posted to radio and gunnery
schools and then to Hamilton Field for training as a back-
seat electronics operator in a P-61 night fighter. After completing school at Hamilton he was again reassigned, this
time to March Field as a radioman in a B-24 training crew.
Shortly before his crew graduated, he was grounded with a
suspected case of spinal meningitis. Two weeks later, the
members of his old crew, along with his replacement, died in
a crash.

His "meningitis," meanwhile, turned out to be something less severe, although never diagnosed. Released from
the hospital, Wheeler received temporary orders to a B-24
flying on submarine patrols off the California coast. The
duty was safe but soporific; on the long flights over water
they often spotted whales but never an enemy sub. He wondered what would happen if they actually encountered one,

for their Liberator carried no depth charges, only sand-filled practice bombs. When the next batch of training crews arrived at March Field he was assigned to Merritt's.

Once the *Liberty Belle* came into range of enemy fighters, Wheeler would move aft from the flight deck and man the left waist gun. Johnson manned the right waist gun. Two other crewmen occupied positions in the after part of the plane. The ball-turret gunner was a nineteen-year-old Minnesotan named Elliott Cunningham. The retractable ball turret lowered into position through an opening in the plane's belly; Cunningham had the unenviable job of hunkering in it, exposed and fetus-like, through most of the flight.

The tail-turret gunner was Gil Carver, from Hoosick, New York. Although his records stated his age as twenty-six, he was actually thirty—a decade older than the other enlisted men in the crew. Carver had lied about his age to enlist in the Air Corps. What amazed the others was that he had chosen to join up when he could have avoided the service altogether, for in addition to being overage for the draft he was married, the father of a four-year-old son, and before enlistment had been working in a defense plant. Why had he ever signed up? Partly, he had succumbed to the near-hysterical patriotism that engulfed the nation following Pearl Harbor—"I saw the flag waving," he said later. Another reason was simple restlessness. He enjoyed the excitement of flying, the camaraderie, and the freedom from domestic constraints.

In the cockpit, Merritt pressed the interphone button and ordered the gunners to test-fire their weapons. Within seconds he heard the distant hammering from the tail turret as Carver opened up, followed by Cunningham in the ball turret and Johnson at the waist position. In the top turret, Corbo squeezed off a jackhammer burst, loosing a cascade of shells onto the flight deck below. Then the nose gunner, Dupree, joined in. An ear-splitting cacophony shook the plane and filled it with the pungent odor of gunsmoke. Every bomber went through the same exercise, collectively donating several tons of lead to the floor of the Adriatic.

Monitoring radio traffic, Merritt heard the pilot of another Liberator report that he was having engine trouble and returning to base. Another followed suit a few minutes later, and another. Of the 335 Liberators and 120 Fortresses that had taken off for Vienna that morning, 60 would ultimately abort the mission because of mechanical difficulties. Keeping the bombers maintained under the brutal conditions of combat was a monumental problem, although the Fifteenth had made great strides during the last year, when the percentage of planes forced home before reaching target had dropped from 40 percent to less than 15.

They were cruising at 190 miles per hour and climbing at a rate of five hundred feet per minute. The altimeter read twelve thousand feet when Merritt ordered the crew to don oxygen masks. Loathed by everyone, the masks were cold and clammy, smelling of rubber and sweat. But they were just one of several discomforts that the crew would endure for the next five hours. Another was the inevitable need to take a leak; so-called relief tubes placed strategically fore and aft were supposed to take care of this, but with temperatures well below zero they often clogged with frozen urine. The high altitude could be devastating in other ways, too. In the unpressurized plane, pockets of gas caught in the intestinal tract could swell like balloons and leave an airman doubled over in pain. The Liberator had no toilet as such,

only a receptacle lined with a wax-paper bag. Anyone desperate enough to use the facility—which meant removing
most of his flight clothes and exposing himself to the arctic
cold—was responsible for disposing of the bag and its contents. This usually meant dropping it out the waist window.
In doing so, care had to be taken that the slipstream didn't
force the bag back inside and splatter its contents throughout the plane.

The formation was at fifteen thousand feet as it crossed
the Dalmatian archipelago near the port of Zara and
changed course to north northeast, cutting across the rugged
landscape of German-occupied Yugoslavia. Off to the right,
a few puffs of gray smoke appeared, gentle reminders from
coastal flak batteries of the far heavier barrage that awaited
them at Vienna. On the ground, everyone along their
route—farmers, soldiers, village children—paused at the
enormous droning and looked skyward at the vast aerial
fleet, whose size and direction were relayed through the
German intelligence network. Once inland, the force would
alter course five times in a series of feints to avoid flak concentrations and to keep the enemy guessing about the target.

Rudolph plotted their progress on his chart and informed
Merritt and Maes of approaching course changes. He
studied the countryside, noting the principal rivers and
towns. As navigator, he was responsible for guiding the
plane, if mortally damaged by enemy fire, to a secure area
before the crew bailed out. Between Italy and Vienna the
most likely haven was Yugoslavia. Although most of that
country was occupied by Germans, pockets of it were controlled by Partisan guerrillas supporting the Allied cause.
The military situation was as fluid as quicksilver, however,
and prior to each mission the navigators were briefed by an

intelligence officer on the current location of friendly forces.

Passing the broad plain of the Sava River, they turned north northwest, climbing to twenty-one thousand feet as they neared the linkup with fighter escort. Rudolph noted that the rendezvous point was near the junction of the Mura and Drava rivers, just north of a town called Koprivnica. At 12:44, right on schedule, a swarm of twin-tailed P-38s and bantam P-51s hove into view, as pretty a sight as a bomber crew ever saw. The fighters waggled their wings in greeting while keeping a respectful distance, for it was not unknown for jumpy gunners to mistake friendly fighters for enemies and open fire.

The escorts took position ahead, above, and on the flanks of the bombers as they crossed into Hungary. They were flying due north now on the penultimate leg of the mission, some six hundred planes arrayed in gleaming chevrons. Everywhere Merritt looked the air was filled with the stepped formations of bombers and fighters. To the right, the long finger of Lake Balaton sprawled across the green landscape of Hungary. Off in the distance on the left, the Alps marched in stately procession. In a final course change, the formation wheeled sixty degrees to the northwest and began climbing to a bombing altitude of twenty-three thousand feet. By one o'clock he could see the twisting Danube and, straddling it upstream on the horizon, Vienna.

They had entered the zone for enemy fighters. Not unexpectedly, but nonetheless to everyone's relief, the sky appeared clear of bogeys. They had heard the grim accounts of Messerschmitts and Folke-Wulfs lined up and attacking head on in deadly phalanx. In the five missions the *Liberty Belle* crew had flown, only on the Munich raid had the remnant Luftwaffe bothered to scramble fighters. Even then, the few that had risen to challenge them had mostly passed Merritt's group to concentrate their fire on looser formations. In the top turret, Corbo had managed to squeeze off a short burst (to no apparent effect) against an ME-109 that cut briefly within range. The most memorable part of that mission had been their first sight, at a mercifully safe distance, of a jet aircraft—the formidable ME-262, which could fly a hundred miles per hour faster than any Allied fighter but whose entry into the war proved too little, too late for German air defense.

Of far greater concern than fighters was the enemy's flak batteries, rendered more deadly by radar. The Germans didn't use radar specifically for aiming their guns (the standard flak defense being a box barrage laid out ahead of the bombers) but rather for fixing the formation's altitude. As a counter-measure, the waist gunners on each plane threw chaff—shredded aluminum foil—out the window. In principle, the descending chaff scattered the radar signals. Chaff came in varying lengths that supposedly corresponded with different radar frequencies, but its benefit may have been more psychological than practical, and with his training in radar theory, Wheeler for one remained openly skeptical about its effectiveness. As they tossed the chaff overboard, he and Johnson were struck by its remarkable resemblance to Christmas-tree tinsel. In fact, they were manufactured by the same companies.

The target could now be seen in the distance. Located six miles downriver from Vienna on a narrow neck of land, the Winterhaven oil depot comprised some fifty storage tanks extending for a mile along the Danube. Since the capture of Ploesti two months earlier by the Russians, smaller oil facilities like Winterhaven, the Lobau refinery across the river (the target of five B-17 groups), and the downstream Nova Schwechat refinery (the third of the day's Vienna targets) had taken on increasing importance in the deteriorating German war effort.

The first wave of Liberators had already turned at the initial point, or I.P., and begun its run on the target. Over the next hour, two hundred and fifty Liberators would unleash five hundred tons of bombs on Winterhaven. Between the bombers and the target lay what looked from a distance like a solid carpet of flak; far below, the airmen could make out the flashes of antiaircraft batteries pumping several thousand rounds a minute into the air, laying a welcome mat of black smoke and screaming metal exactly at the formation's altitude. Black cumulus, the bomber crews called it. From his perch in the top turret of the *Liberty Belle*, Corbo wondered wishfully if the billowing black puffs might actually be storm clouds.

The first bombs had found their mark, turning parts of the target into a roiling inferno of flame and smoke. Four miles above the conflagration, vignettes of mayhem and carnage were playing themselves out in the flak-pocked sky. A plane in the lead bomb group was the first casualty, sliding out of formation with two engines on fire. Minutes later, another Liberator lost half a wing, flipped on its back and went into a mortal spin. Another took a hit directly amidships, plunging earthward with such force that both wings sheared off. Like a broken piñata, another split in half at the bombbay, spilling crewmen as it fell. So it went for the next fifty minutes as the formations pressed on.

Below them, the crewmen of the *Liberty Belle* watched the blossoming parachutes drift down through the flak field. They had rounded the I.P. and with the other four boxes in their group set a straight course for the target. It was 1:32 P.M. Now that they were actually on the bomb run, control of the aircraft passed to Martin and the Norden bombsight, which was linked to the autopilot so that the bombardier actually steered the plane onto the target. The Norden consisted of a telescopic sight and a mechanical computer that factored in relative wind speed and direction and the plane's altitude to calculate the point of release. For Martin and most of the other bombardiers in the group, however, lining up the target was mainly an exercise, for standard procedure called for them to keep their eyes on the lead plane and to toggle their bombs the instant its bombardier released his.

Chatter on the interphone had ceased as soon as the *Liberty Belle* rounded the I.P. and proceeded toward the wall of flak lying directly ahead. They were on the run for nine interminable minutes before somebody broke the sweaty silence: "All hell's going to break loose any minute." Suddenly they were inside the flak zone, cruising through a sea of shell bursts opening like delicate black flowers in a time-lapse film. The sound, a muffled "whoomp . . . whoomp," was curiously gentle. Red flame licked at the core of nearby bursts that sent fragments of steel rattling against the *Liberty Belle* skin like sleet against a window pane. Miraculously, as they approached the target, all twenty-seven planes in the group navigated the flak field without a casualty. At last the lead plane let go its bombs. Martin pressed the toggle switch on cue, and the *Liberty Belle* surged with the release of her two-ton load.

Merritt banked the plane steeply to the left and headed toward the rally point and home. In the top turret, Corbo breathed easy and said to himself: "We've made this one." The thought had no sooner flashed through his mind than the *Liberty Belle* shuddered from the impact of three or possibly four nearly direct hits. In the cockpit, a piece of shrapnel exploded through the flight deck and blew out one of the Plexiglas panels overhead. Merritt fought the wheel as the plane heaved and slowed to the brink of stalling; then she began dropping while the engines screamed out of control and the rest of the formation pulled away. Gently, he pushed the wheel forward to pick up some speed while Maes extended the landing flaps to increase lift.

Shrapnel had ripped through all four engines with varying degrees of damage. The left outboard engine, number one, coughed and died immediately. As it did, Maes hit one of the nickel-sized buttons on the panel in front of him to feather its windmilling prop, which slowed and stopped as it turned parallel to the slipstream. The oil and manifold pressure gauges for the number-two engine read low, but it seemed to be doing all right. On the right-hand side, smoke and flame poured from the cowling of number three. Maes punched a button activating a remote CO_2 extinguisher and kept on pressing until the fire was out. The number-four engine raced wildly, its governor blown away, but by adjusting the propeller's pitch he was able to get it more or less under control.

Although stabilized, none of the three remaining engines were giving anywhere near full power, and their combined output could not have equaled much more than one good engine. They whined in a deafening caterwaul, their props wildly out of synch, while fuel streamed from the riddled wing tanks, filling the plane with the reek of gasoline.

Elsewhere in the plane, the other crewmen were coping as well as possible. In the waist section, the force of the three explosions had knocked Johnson and Wheeler to the deck. Johnson was up quickly and signaled to Carver in the tail and Cunningham in the ball turret. On the interphone he reported to Merritt that everyone in the after part of the plane was okay.

Shrapnel had cut communications to the nose section, but despite damage to the compartment, Martin and Dupree were all right. Inches behind Martin, a fist-sized piece of flak had blown out the retracted nose wheel and exploded several oxygen tanks, but he had remained untouched. Rudolph was nowhere to be seen—Martin assumed he had gone back to the flight deck. The plane had obviously been hit but seemed under control. Martin poked his head into the navigator's dome and glanced back at the cockpit, wiping his forehead in a mock gesture as if to say, "Whew— we made it!" Only when he saw the frantic looks on the faces of Maes and Merritt did he realize they were in trouble. He rapped on the door of the nose turret to alert Dupree, who appeared collected even though shrapnel had ripped through the Plexiglas just over his head.

"Get your G.I. shoes on," Martin told him. "We may be bailing out."

Within five minutes after clearing the target, the *Liberty Belle* had dropped to twelve thousand feet and was still losing altitude. To lighten her they began jettisoning ammunition, flak vests, helmets, oxygen bottles—anything not bolted down. Responding grudgingly, the plane slowed its rate of descent. They were still over Austria and vulnerable to any Luftwaffe patrols looking for easy prey. Merritt tried calling for fighter escort, but the radio was dead. Over the interphone, he told Wheeler to check the radio equipment space above the wing root to see if he could repair the transmitter—a futile exercise, as it turned out, as well as unnecessary, for minutes later two P-51s appeared out of nowhere and took station on the *Liberty Belle*'s flanks, guardian angels flying so close that Merritt could see the pilot's faces. They were black. The tails and wingtips of both Mustangs were painted red, the color of the 332nd all-Negro fighter group, one of several segregated units of the Fifteenth Air Force.

He had never been happier to see anyone, black or white, in his life. The Mustangs stayed with them for half an hour until low fuel forced them back to base. By then, the *Liberty Belle* was safely beyond the Luftwaffe's range.

As the Mustangs veered toward home and disappeared into the distance, the *Liberty Belle* continued south over western Hungary. The plane slushed along, while Merritt and Maes together fought the controls to hold her steady. They passed the blue crescent of Lake Balaton off to the left. Preoccupied with keeping the plane aloft, Merritt was surprised to notice how beautiful the lake appeared as it shimmered in the afternoon sun.

The *Liberty Belle* was still losing altitude, although more slowly than before. It had been an hour and a lifetime since coming through the flak. More gliding than flying now, she limped across the Drava River into Yugoslavia. Checking landmarks against his chart, Rudolph noted where the Mura River flowed into the Drava from the west; south of this junction was the town of Koprivnica. According to his intelligence briefing that morning, in another few minutes they would pass over Partisan-held territory. The *Liberty Belle* was at two thousand feet now, lower than the mountains off to her right, and nearly out of fuel when Merritt told the crew to prepare to jump. As they approached a range of hills west of the town, he switched on the interphone again:

"Bail out and good luck."

Chapter 2
THE QUEST

The last thing Wheeler knew, he had been in the back of the plane, kneeling on the deck and clutching the rim of the open camera hatch, fixed on the green and yellow landscape rolling by, so close it seemed that he could reach out and touch it. He held fast to the rim. The hatch seemed so small, barely big enough to squeeze his head and shoulders through. What had they said in training about bailing out? Lunge headfirst through the hatch and toward the front of the plane. Don't pull the ripcord until you've straightened your legs and are well clear of the plane. . . .

Suddenly the hills were no longer framed by the open hatch but were spread out before him. Loosed from his grip on the plane, he lay sprawled on the wind. He could hear, above the sound of air rushing through his flight helmet, the receding drone of engines.

Someone had booted him out of the plane.

Son of a bitch!

Instinctively he grabbed for the ripcord handle and pulled. He heard the chute pop, the nylon hissing out behind him and almost instantly the *Whuump!* of the canopy as it blossomed with air, wrenching him from freefall. He reached for the parachute straps to control his swing. Suspended over the soft, undulant hills, he heard machine-gun fire and noticed, off in the distance, people running up a ridge. The thought flashed through his mind that he was coming down in the midst of a combat training exercise. As the ground moved closer he saw clearings amidst the trees, a few houses, and coming up fast now a sloping vineyard with rows of grape stakes and a cart path between them.

He hit in the middle of the path, next to a scrubby tree. The ground struck hard and sent him tumbling, but he was on his feet quickly and soon had the parachute balled up and unstrapped. The day was warm, and he began to strip off his flight clothes. When he threw off his gloves he realized that he had somehow cut one of his hands. He stared at the hand—a messy, disembodied thing, besmeared with blood, which had already begun to dry. It seemed to belong to someone else. He felt no pain and couldn't see where he was cut. Tend to it later. With his good hand he unzipped his flight suit and fumbled through his escape kit for maps.

He assumed they had landed somewhere in Austria or Yugoslavia. There were two maps in the escape kit: one for Scandinavia, the other for northern Germany.

A lot of good these will do me!

It occurred to him to find the rest of the crew. He was wondering in what direction to go when he saw three women approaching on the path. He jumped at the sight of them—he'd heard stories of peasant women in Germany and Austria attacking downed airmen with pitchforks—but their demeanor suggested they were friendly.

"American!" he exclaimed. When one of them noticed his bloody hand, she left and returned with a pan of water and began washing it.

Warmed by the autumn sun, he surrendered to the ministrations of the woman who knelt beside him, talking quietly with the others in a language he couldn't identify. She was dressing the hand with gauze from his escape kit when he heard yelling and this time saw a man running up the hillside, waving a revolver.

Jesus!

He sprang to his feet and reached for the service automatic in his shoulder holster, then thought better of it. The man was older, a civilian; he looked alarmed, as though someone were chasing him. He motioned for Wheeler to pick up his flight suit and parachute and to follow him.

■

Art Johnson came down in the top of a high tree. He managed to swing onto a branch and unbuckle his parachute, then climbed down to the last limb. He still had about thirty feet to go. Embracing the trunk, he half slid, half fell the rest of the way, hitting the ground so hard that he blacked out for a minute. Coming to, he felt a sharp pain in his back but did his best to ignore it as he proceeded along a wooded path toward some houses he'd seen from the tree. He moved cautiously, stopping every twenty yards or so to look around and listen. When he heard someone coming up the path, he unclicked the safety on his automatic and slipped into some underbrush. Peering through the brush, Johnson saw approaching him a man dressed in civilian clothes, carrying a rifle and walking in a fast crouch, eyes alert. The man spotted Johnson right away.

"*Americanski,*" he whispered, and motioned for the airman to follow him.

■

Coming down on the edge of the woods, Carl Rudolph braced for landing—legs together, knees bent, arms in front of his face, just as they had taught him in training. His legs collapsed as he hit, and for a moment he lost his breath but was otherwise okay. He stepped out of his harness and tried to free the parachute from some branches; when it refused to budge, he abandoned it and started down a path. Checking the dime-sized brass compass from his escape kit, he headed in a northeasterly direction, following the line of descent in hopes of picking up other crewmen. After a few minutes he saw, coming in the opposite direction, a group of peasant women and children, led by a shabbily dressed older man with a big moustache and his arm raised in greeting.

Not knowing what else to do, Rudolph smiled, declared himself "American," and shook the man's hand. The Yugoslav grinned broadly under his moustache as the women and children rushed past them and tugged the chute free from the tree. Another man, this one younger, with a rifle and dressed in a gray wool uniform and a forage cap with a red star on it—the symbol of the Communist Partisans, about whom he had been briefed by intelligence officers—came running up the hill out of breath and indicated for Rudolph to follow.

They started off in a trot and found Cunningham, the ball-turret gunner, hiding in the brush near the stream where he had landed. He joined in the jog, and soon Johnson and his Partisan became part of the group, too. The afternoon was hot. Shedding their flight coveralls, they walked and ran for the next two hours. At last they came to a break in the trees. One of the Partisans motioned them to get low and follow fast across the clearing to some standing corn about two hundred yards away. They stopped to rest there. As they sat panting in the shade of the rustling stalks, their guide pointed in the direction from which they'd come.

"*Germanski*," he said, then pointing ahead in the direction they would be going: "*Partizane*."

■

Nick Corbo fell into the trees not far from a vineyard where some women, children, and older men were harvesting grapes. More in wonder than in fear, they quickly surrounded him as he struggled to free his parachute from the tree. They were obviously friendly, and when he indicated by gestures that he was thirsty, one of them offered him a bottle of a clear liquid. He took a big slug. It wasn't water, that was for sure, for it burned all the way down and left a pleasant warmth in his stomach. He'd never felt so thirsty; anything liquid was good. He took another belt.

■

Keith Martin, the bombardier, was the first one out of the forward part of the plane. He landed in a vineyard, nearly impaling himself on a grape stake.

His descent was short and fast, his parachute having failed to open on the first few tugs of the ripcord. He kicked away the sharpened stake and hit the ground with a thud, his fall softened by the cultivated earth. Yanking off his parachute harness, he headed down a path and had gone less than a hundred yards when he found Corbo, waving the bottle he'd been given and shouting, "Lieutenant Martin! Lieutenant Martin!"

"Corbo—get the hell down and shut up!"

They got off the path and moved into the woods; Martin remembered a briefing officer saying that the Germans avoided the woods for fear of Partisan units operating there. Once they had gone far enough into the forest to feel safe, he fired a shot into the air to attract attention. Corbo did the same. Several shots later, a voice shouted _Stoy_! They heard rustling and glanced around; almost magically, the woods were filled with uniformed men with assault rifles leveled in their direction.

■

Don Maes, the second-to-last man out of the _Liberty Belle_, came down at the edge of the woods. He rolled when he hit, and as he pushed himself up he was startled by something black and alive under his nose. It was a salamander, slithering through the dead leaves.

■

Merritt was the last one to jump. Like Martin's, his chute refused to open on the first few pulls of the ripcord. When at last it billowed above him, he was probably five hundred feet from the ground. Descending, he watched the _Liberty Belle_ arc to the left as it skidded into a slow, majestic circle. He worried for a moment that the plane might circle all the way around and entangle him or one of the other crewmen in the line of swinging parachutes, but there wasn't enough life left in her for that. Like a crippled goose, the bomber skimmed the treetops and plunged headlong into a ravine. He watched in awe as the plane disintegrated, the wings shearing and the engines tumbling down the slope. The rending sound of wood and metal was followed by the roar of the explosion. The hot air from the fireball lifted him in his chute.

Moments later he was into the trees. The chute caught in the branches, jerking him to a stop a long leap short of the ground. He cut the shrouds, dropped the rest of the way, and headed up the line of descent to collect the other crewmen.

He found Maes burying his chute in the leaves. They got out their escape kits and were poring over a map of Yugoslavia when they heard someone coming and crouched behind a bush. They drew their service automatics and unclicked the safeties. Through the brush they saw, approaching along the edge of the woods, two men carrying rifles and wearing gray wool caps with red stars.

■

Ivan Serbec, age thirty-nine and by occupation a coal miner, was helping in the grape harvest in the vineyards over-looking his village of Subotica when he heard the plane approaching. Earlier in the afternoon he had stood in the vineyard, watching the waves of bombers returning from their strikes in the north. Now a straggler from that group was coming in low over the trees. He could tell by its height and speed and by the sound of the engines that it was in trouble. It sputtered overhead, close enough for him to see men in it. A startling sight! Without thinking about the absurdity of the gesture, he took off his cap and waved. Then the men began falling from the plane, and a line of parachutes materialized in the hazy sky.

The bomber disappeared over the ridge. When Serbec heard the explosion, he took off up the hill. Upon reaching the edge of the woods he found several members of the Partisan territorial patrol—Stjepan Prlog, Svagelj Branko, and Vincek Valent—already there with two airmen. Valent had lived for a while in America, and between his limited English and sign language they were able to assure the airmen that they had fallen into friendly hands. Serbec and the others were pleased to learn that the two airmen were the pilots of the downed plane; it pleased them even more when one of the Americans (Maes) gave them his parachute and pistol with a full magazine of bullets.

"We must hurry," said Valent. "You come with us."

■

On the sun-washed morning of September 5, 1986, two cars drove along a gravel road in northeastern Croatia. I was at the wheel of the second car, a small but serviceable Fiat that my father and I had rented in Zagreb. It was Friday, our fourth day in Yugoslavia. The lead car carried an editor from the local newspaper, as well as an officer from the veteran's club of nearby Koprivnica and a man who was supposedly guiding us to the spot, somewhere up on the wooded ridge ahead, where the *Liberty Belle* had met its fiery end exactly forty-one years, eleven months and two days before.

We pulled off the highway and onto a secondary road that skirted a pasture. Bright blue chicory flowers, daisies, and Queen Anne's lace lined the shoulder, nodding in the wake of the car ahead. A rusty metal sign informed us that we were coming to Vrhovic, the place where the *Liberty Belle* crewmen had spent their first night in Yugoslavia. Vrhovic showed on our map as a village, but only a cartographer's leap of faith made it so; it appeared to be nothing more than three or four farmhouses along the road.

We pulled over. Edi Selhaus, our host and the man most responsible for our being there in Yugoslavia, wanted a photograph of my father posing next to the sign. Dad obliged, and at Edi's request he held up a piece of paper with the years "1944–1986" written on it. Dad smiled gamely as Edi snapped away. My father is reticent by nature, and I was not altogether sure that he was enjoying this much attention. Since arriving in Yugoslavia he had been a walking media event; reporters, photographers, and a television news crew had followed us everywhere to record the return of the American airman.

Back at the car, we proceeded up the road and stopped at a white-washed house with chickens and turkeys foraging in the yard. A middle-aged woman in a striped shirt greeted us with a warm smile that flashed gold fillings. Janez Zerovc, our co-host and translator, did the introductions. Although too young to have participated in the events of 1944, the woman had an uncle, now deceased, who used to tell her about the bomber—or "boomer," as Janez pronounced it—crashing not far from here. Some parts of the plane salvaged by the uncle had remained in the family, and she showed them to us now. One of them was a gear the size of a dinner plate, the other a metal tube about as big as my arm. My father examined these strange heirlooms while the woman looked on proudly and cameras clicked. He identified the tube as part of the wheel strut but shrugged when asked about the gear. Janez, a World War II airplane buff, was confident that it had been part of the mechanism for changing the propeller pitch.

The parts fascinated me, but by now we had visited several homes where relics of the *Liberty Belle* had been retrieved from the attics for our benefit. I wanted to get to the crash site and was glad when we moved on. A mile or so farther up the hill, we stopped again to parlay. The talk was all in Serbo-Croatian and well beyond the meager facility I had gleaned from studying the language at home during the previous few months. There appeared to be some uncertainty about our itinerary. Janez, my father, and I remained in the car while Edi and the others deliberated. Dad began to doze in the back seat. Next to me in the front, Janez shook his head as he waited for the discussion to conclude.

"Edi is very . . . What is the word? *Politic*," he said.

"You mean he likes to talk."

"Yes. Sometimes he is too much politic."

At last the group broke up and Edi returned to the car. "We go back," he said.

■

Singly and in groups of twos and threes, the *Liberty Belle* crewmen made their way down the hillside. They stopped frequently to allow their Partisan guides to reconnoiter the territory ahead. In all, they covered only a couple of miles, but with such caution that it was nearly dusk by the time they were at last reassembled. Rudolph, Johnson, and Cunningham got to the village first and were plied with a clear plum brandy by the local populace, who stood around gawking at the Americans. After a few stiff swigs of this limpid lightning, Rudolph's self-consciousness dissolved. Following libations, they devoured a dinner of thin soup, stringy smoked ham, and black bread.

Between sign language, a little English, and some German, the Americans and Yugoslavs managed to make themselves understood to one another. The main concern of Merritt and the rest of the crew was the whereabouts of Gil Carver, the tail gunner. The Partisans gave conflicting reports on his fate. One of them said he had been captured, another that he had been wounded and captured, another that he was dead—killed by the local Croatian fascists, the *Ustashi*. To emphasize the point, the Partisan drew his fingers across his throat, a universal sign whose meaning no one missed.

But who actually knew? As they would discover again and again over the next few weeks, none of the Partisans spoke with any real authority; not about Carver, or where they were going, or how they were going to get out of here.

■

We pulled into the yard of a stucco house and were greeted by the barking of a scruffy German shepherd on a chain. The mistress of the house, a woman who looked in her mid-forties, came out onto the flower-bedecked porch and shook hands with Janez and Edi, whom she obviously had met before. A boy of about five huddled close to her, watching us with curious eyes. A much older woman dressed from head to toe in black joined them on the porch. She was probably eighty years old, with strong peasant features framed by a shawl.

Janez explained to us that the old woman had lived in this house during the war and remembered the Americans staying here—three in the house and the others, perhaps, in the barn or at another farmhouse nearby. My father looked at the house and the adjacent barn (really just a hay mow), but nothing either here or at a neighboring house sparked any recollection.

We wandered back to the road, where Edi was engaged in an animated discussion with several farmers. One of them wore a strapped undershirt and held a pitchfork. The other leaned precariously on a scythe; he was about sixty, with a week-old stubble covering his gaunt face, and long gone in the bottle. He poked a stick at a map drawn in the dirt— they were debating again the best route to the crash site. Everyone seemed to have an equally strong conviction. Arms waved and the Serbo-Croatian flew.

This is a Mediterranean culture, I told myself, and we have to take it on its own terms. My father, who is perhaps the least Mediterranean person I know, stood well to one side, hands in pocket, waiting for the debate to conclude.

At last we were on our way again. But to our dismay, instead of heading up the road we returned to the house where we had stopped earlier to examine the plane parts. Protocol required us to go inside for the inevitable coffee klatch and round of *rakija*, the same plum-based whiskey that had fortified the *Liberty Belle* crewmen forty-two years before. At eleven o'clock in the morning it can be a little hard to handle, but after three days in Yugoslavia I was get-ting used to it.

There were eight of us squeezed around the little table in the dark, paneled dining room. The room was small and claustrophobic. The hostess had set before us not only

coffee and *rakija* but beer, wine, mineral water, and cookies.
As the conversation warmed, it became apparent that we
were going to be stuck here for a while. Janez didn't bother
to translate, and I sensed that he was as impatient as my dad
and I to get moving.

As the talk and laughter flowed, my mind replayed the
beginning of our improbable adventure.

■

In the eyes of a son, a father's war stories take on the quality
of myth. Growing up, I heard my dad speak often of his last
mission and his subsequent forty-nine days as a downed
airman in Yugoslavia. A persistent memory from my childhood is sitting in the attic of our house, in Montclair, New
Jersey, amid packets of letters, faded newspaper clippings,
service records, and other mementos of my parents' wartime
years. One item in particular compelled my attention: the
yellowed Western Union telegram, creased sharply at the
fold, with its cryptic message in large block letters.

THE SECRETARY OF WAR DESIRES ME TO EXPRESS HIS
DEEP REGRET THAT YOUR HUSBAND FIRST LIEUTENANT
JOHN I MERRITT HAS BEEN REPORTED MISSING IN
ACTION SINCE SEVEN OCTOBER OVER AUSTRIA IF FUR-
THER DETAILS OR OTHER INFORMATION ARE RECEIVED
YOU WILL BE PROMPTLY NOTIFIED.

The boy who sat there cross-legged on the attic floor,
poring over these tersely bureaucratic words by the light of a
bare bulb, couldn't have been older than eight or nine; old
enough, anyhow, to realize the impact those words must

have had on my mother, who was twenty-four when she read them and living with me and my sister and grandmother in Texas. I sensed, however dimly, the bond created between my mother and father by the shared experience of wartime separation, a bond that drew them closer to themselves, perhaps, than they could ever be with anyone else. When I first became aware of those events of 1944, they had taken place less than ten years before. From my childhood perspective, however, it might as well have been a century. In those musty attic papers and in television documentaries like *Victory at Sea*, World War II seemed as remote as Gettysburg or Armageddon, an island in time inhabited long ago by my parents.

They were barely out of their twenties then, and too busy building their future to dwell on the past. My father was working as a lift-truck salesman, a job that took him on the road so that he was often home only on weekends. My sense of those wartime years was derived as much from my maternal grandmother, who lived with us throughout my childhood. It was she who had dreamed, on a night in December 1944, that my father was safe. The next day my mother received word that he had made it back to Italy. By Christmas he was home. I was eight months old at the time and had been living amidst a gaggle of females—my mother, sister, grandmother, and aunt; for all intents and purposes I had never seen my father, who had left for training and overseas duty within a fortnight of my birth. It is part of family lore that when he walked through the door on his return, I screamed.

Another link to those days was my father's Army Air Corps uniform. It hung in a walk-in closet off my parents' bedroom, a beautiful artifact with pants of khaki twill and a fitted olive jacket set off by the embroidered arm patch of the Fifteenth Air Force, silver lieutenant's bars and pilot's wings, and a double row of ribbons that included a Distinguished Flying Cross. Carl Rudolph, my father's navigator and his best friend among the crew, lived nearby. Every October, on the anniversary of their Vienna mission, my dad, mother, and Rudy and his wife went out to dinner. At least once during my boyhood I recall them donning their old uniforms for the occasion. As they left for the evening they were laughing at the reaction they anticipated from the other restaurant patrons. It is a celebration of survival they continued for more than forty years.

■

In describing this annual rite of the Merritts and Rudolphs, I don't wish to give the impression that my father was (or is) the type to sit around an American Legion hall telling war stories. He's a man living very much in the present. At the time of these events he was an executive still several years from retirement, who had guided the expansion of a small family real-estate firm into one of the major development companies on the East Coast. He's tough, decisive, self-confident: qualities I envied, in part because I had often felt so lacking in them myself.

My own temperament—at the risk of sounding precious I'll call it literary and reflective—couldn't be more different. In college I had majored in English; upon graduation, in part to avoid being drafted into the Army and sent to Vietnam, I joined the Navy. I wound up in Vietnam anyway, but only briefly, in safe duty as an officer aboard a destroyer escort patrolling the coast. Later I went into newspaper work and

eventually wound up in a public relations job at my alma
mater, Princeton University. Avocationally, I pursued free-
lance magazine writing and wrote a book about the American West.

By December 1984 I had completed the book, my first,
and had begun pondering the possibility of a second. Sooner
than I might have thought, an idea for a subject suggested
itself. My wife and I and our two teen-age daughters were
having dinner with my parents on New Year's Eve when a
remark by one of my daughters prompted some recollection
on my dad's part about his sojourn in Yugoslavia.

"I wonder if there's a book possibility in this Yugoslavia
business?" I said. "How much more do you think we could
find out about what happened there?"

The notion intrigued him. However, in discussing the
prospect, it was apparent that we would be starting from the
slimmest of knowledge bases. My father had stayed in touch
with only two of his nine crewmen and during his stay in
Yugoslavia had kept no diary or notes. With the years, the
memory of those events had distilled down to a few anec-
dotes.

"Maybe I could get you and Rudy together to reminisce,
and a lot of this stuff would come back," I suggested.

"I'll talk to him and see if I can get him over sometime in
the next couple of weeks," he said.

He seemed interested, and I wanted to take this initial
step despite some immediate reservations. For one thing, the
possibility of collecting enough information for a book
seemed remote. For another, I had been trying to focus my
writing efforts on certain well-defined subjects, and World
War II was miles from the terrain I had chosen to plow. I
worried, too, about probing into my parents' personal life

and going beyond the boundaries my father and I had established in our comfortable, if somewhat superficial, relationship.

These thoughts were running through my mind several weeks later, on a bright winter Saturday morning, as I drove to my parents' house, an hour and ten minutes away in northern New Jersey. As planned, my father had arranged for Rudy to join us to talk about their last mission and seven weeks in Yugoslavia. I was a little ahead of Rudy, and my ambivalence melted as soon as he arrived. He carried a leather folder and was wearing a checkered wool shirt and a big grin. It had probably been twenty-five years since I had last seen him, but when he walked through the door he appeared hardly to have aged at all. Several years younger than my dad, he was sixty-two and on the verge of retiring from his engineering job; he and his wife were looking forward to selling their suburban house and moving permanently to the New Jersey shore. Part of my reaction toward Rudy's youthfulness, of course, was due to my own changing perspective on age. The previous April I had turned forty, a point in life when sixty can look downright coltish; I was now older by a few years than Rudy had been the last time we'd met, and older by nearly a generation than Rudy and my dad during World War II.

Rudy's folder contained several items, including a gray wool forage cap, which he placed jauntily on his head. "*Pilote*," he said, grinning at my dad. He pronounced the word pee-LOTE—as I would learn, this was the Serbo-Croatian word for "pilot" and the designation the Partisans invariably used in singling out my father from the rest of the crew.

He removed the cap and handed it to me. "A gift from

the Partisans. They made these things out of blankets. It came with a red star on it, but I took it off right away. I didn't want the Germans thinking I was a Partisan if they captured me."

Next he showed me a large brass D-ring. "Can you guess what this is?" he asked, grasping the ring and holding it to his chest. It was the ripcord handle, salvaged from his parachute in the frantic moments after landing and kept on the trek across Yugoslavia and down all the years.

The D-ring recalled my dad's experience when he jumped. "The first two times I pulled the ripcord nothing happened," he said. "It felt like the cable was stuck. I must have been falling for about ten seconds and figured I had time for one more good yank. I grabbed it with both hands and pulled like hell and the damn thing finally popped. I was the last one out and the first to hit the ground." When he gave the order to bail out, he remembered, the plane was flying at about two thousand feet. "Cunningham, our armorer and ball-turret gunner, came on the interphone and said that Wheeler, the radioman, wouldn't jump. I called back, 'Boot him out!' and they did." Even with this delay, he added, "it all happened real fast. I think everyone was out of the plane within thirty seconds after I gave the order to jump."

Rudy had brought a sheath of papers with him. As he spread them out on the dining-room table, I recognized an item from my father's cache of wartime memorabilia, a copy of the March Field *Beacon*, the newspaper of his bomber crew's California training command, with a front-page story proclaiming them "crew of the week" and pictures of each crewman superimposed on a photograph of a B-24.

But it was Rudy's other materials that excited me. Laid

out before me was a large map of northern Yugoslavia. It was identical to the one carried in Rudy's escape kit and had been carefully annotated, with their route marked with a dashed pencil line. Even more valuable was a twenty-page manuscript on faded yellow legal paper. Written in pencil with the title "The Walk Back" across the top of the first page, it had been drafted by Rudy within a month after their return from Yugoslavia. "It's been twenty years since I looked at this stuff," he said.

Until now, my knowledge of their Yugoslavia experience had consisted of a handful of disconnected stories related to me in childhood and centering on my father—a slim codex whose entire text would scarcely fill a paragraph. As my dad and Rudy studied the map and read through the manuscript, memories came pouring back. Here now were incidents linked to dates and places and details of their final mission, the bailout, and day-to-day life in Yugoslavia. In reconstructing their story, I would now have more to go on than the vagaries of memory.

■

The interview and Rudy's materials were an encouraging start. The next obvious step would be to track down any government documents that might be available. I wrote the U.S. Air Force Archives, located at Maxwell Air Force Base, in Alabama. I knew that on their return to Italy, the crewmen had been interviewed by intelligence officers in Bari, and I hoped that perhaps the debriefing report might be on file, along with records kept by the Fifteenth Air Force of its operations for October 7, 1944. Within a month after writing Maxwell for information, I received a thick packet of photocopied papers, a documentary trove that included mission summaries for my father's 304th Bomb Wing, with numbers of aircraft, bomb loads, and weather and course data for his last mission.

Further correspondence led me to the military affairs division of National Archives, depository of the missing air crew reports routinely filed whenever a plane failed to return from a mission. Researchers there were able to locate the report on my dad's crew, and for a five-dollar fee I obtained a microfiche copy. The microfiche was a three-by-five-inch acetate card with five neat rows of squares. Peering at the squares through a magnifying glass, I saw they were pages from official-looking documents. At the first opportunity, I took the card to Firestone Library, at Princeton, to read it on a viewing machine.

As I adjusted the dials on the machine the first page leapt into focus. It was a standard form with the words "Confidential—missing air crew report" across the top. The report was dated October 10, 1944 (three days after the mission) and gave the name of the missing plane; this was my first knowledge that it had been called the *Liberty Belle*, which my dad and Rudy hadn't mentioned and had presumably forgotten. The report included a freehand map of the Vienna area with an "X" indicating the plane's last observed position, a few miles south of the city. Other appendices—statements by my dad and other members of the crew which obviously had been added later—dealt with Carver, the missing tail gunner:

> *Carver bailed out, his chute did open and he returned a wave to one of the other men on his way down. Approximately thirty minutes after I landed, the co-*

pilot and I heard a good many shots from small arms about one half a mile away lasting about five minutes. Soon after we were picked up by Partisans, and the next morning we were told that Sgt. Carver had been taken by the Ustashi, some Partisans saying he had been shot, others that he had been only captured.

Sgt. Carver was seen going down in his parachute & in good condition, never seen of since. Patisians reported him killed by Utashi.

Carver's chute was seen to open. Never seen on ground. Partizans said he was captured, later said he was dead. Didn't seem to have any clear information as to what happened to him.

The last page was a brief statement, undated and unsigned, in apparent response to a follow-up query after the war:

I have since heard from Gilman Carver by letter and he said he had been captured but was liberated by the Americans when they took Germany. He was then sent to a hospital in England and has since returned to U.S. I belive he has been discharged now. So if this questionare has been sent in the belief that some member of our crew is still missing, you had better check the records.

To my surprise, the microfiche contained four other missing air crew reports, including those for two other B-24s lost on the same mission of October 7. The first of these concerned a Liberator piloted by a Lieutenant Lavoid Wagner. His plane was one of the first over the target and was hit by flak only seconds before bombs-away. The plane fell back from the rest of the formation and began to veer out of control, but Wagner had her flying steadily again once the bombardier salvoed his two-ton load of bombs. The plane limped home safely, but minus four crewmen who had bailed out during the first moments after being hit.

Other pages of Wagner's file filled in the rest of the story. An airman in a nearby formation reported seeing the four missing crewmen's parachutes open in the center of the flak field. Another page listed their names and next-of-kin. The last page in the file repeated the four names on a form that momentarily confused me. Examining the form closely, I saw that it was printed in German and must have been a report conveyed through the Red Cross. Among the few words I recognized were "Stalag Luft"; the four airmen, I realized, had survived their descent through the flak and had been interned in a Luftwaffe prisoner-of-war camp.

The other report for October 7 described the fate of a B-24 nicknamed *White K*, piloted by Second Lieutenant Oscar Rambeck. Three airmen in nearby Liberators gave slightly varying accounts of the same grim scene. A direct hit severed the left wing of *White K*, flipping the plane over and sending it, according to an eyewitness, into "a tight death spiral . . . No chutes were seen to open."

I puzzled a few moments over the last page of the report. It was another form, undated and titled "Casualty Questionnaire," with the usual list of queries: Where did your aircraft strike the ground? What members of your crew were in the aircraft when it struck the ground? Where were they in the aircraft? What was their condition?

The respondent, a Sergeant John Kulenics, of Canton, Ohio, had answered to each of these, "No knowledge."

To the question, Did you bail out? he replied:

> *No knowledge*
> *I believe i was blown out.*

A final entry stated:

> *A german doctor came into the lager where i was being held and asked everyone in the group whether or not we knew a Johnson which was the name of my Co-Pilot however he did not mention any given name of course we did not say anything to the fact that we knew him. By the way the lager was in Vienna. Now this may have been my Co-Pilot and it may not have been.*

It was not. Kulenics, it dawned on me, was *White K*'s sole survivor, miraculously thrown from his top-turret position the instant the plane flipped and began its harrowing plunge, carrying nine young men to their deaths four miles below.

Realizing that documents like these would allow me to reconstruct the entire Vienna mission, I wrote Maxwell Air Force Base and the National Archives for additional materials. Soon I had a manila envelope full of transparencies; by the light of the microfiche screen I pored through more tales of terror and death at twenty-three thousand feet.

A Liberator piloted by a Major James Murray was the afternoon's first casualty, receiving nearly simultaneous hits that knocked out two engines and killed one of the waist gunners. Two crewmen bailed out of the top hatch as the plane slid into a dive; two others, Sergeants Daniel Posner and Robert Wood, were thrown out of the rear hatch when the pilot pulled up suddenly on the controls. The rest bailed out south of the city and were captured, but Posner and Wood were never found.

Lieutenant Harvey Robinett's plane took a direct hit over the target. He and four others—the copilot, navigator, bombardier, and left waist gunner—parachuted safely and were taken prisoner. The remaining five crewmen went down with the plane.

Flak caught the Liberator piloted by Lieutenant Rudolf Lunak amidships just after bombs away. The copilot of the plane behind Lunak's saw the tail gunner slump forward over his guns, which began firing wildly as the bomber slipped into a violent spin that sheared off the wings. Shrapnel ripped through the legs of waist gunner David Feheley. He passed out and woke up in midair, tore off his flak vest, and pulled the ripcord before passing out again. Waking up on the ground, he found himself in the back of a moving truck, a prisoner of war headed for a military hospital. Feheley, the only one of the ten-man crew to make it out of the plane alive, survived his ordeal but lost both legs.

Lieutenant Arden Herkimer's plane took two direct hits. One blew out the front turret, killing the gunner and throwing him back onto the bombardier, who was flung from the plane as it lurched into a steep spiral and split in two. In the cockpit, the force of the spin jammed the copilot into his seat. Herkimer and the top-turret gunner, Robert Malby, struggled to free him but couldn't. "You'd better get out," he said calmly. They did, Herkimer jumping from the bombbay, Malby going out the top hatch. Malby's chute opened, but he was never seen again and may have been killed by his own turret guns, their trigger jammed in firing position. Unable to unstrap himself from his seat, the copilot—a substitute crewman flying his first mission—went down with the plane.

Besides the *Liberty Belle*, four other bombers hit over the target managed to limp back as far as Yugoslavia before their crews bailed out. Two crews were rescued by Partisans and evacuated to Italy—one after a few days in-country, the other after six weeks. The two other planes made it to the Allied-held island of Vis, a sanctuary for crippled bombers off the Dalmatian coast. The pilots hoped to land at Vis but instead ordered their crews to jump because of a crippled plane blocking the runway. Twenty parachutes blossomed over the island. Strong winds blew eleven of the men out to sea; all but two drowned.

Overall, the records for the mission of October 7, 1944, to Vienna showed that, of 390 bombers to reach the target, 14 failed to return. Of approximately thirty-nine hundred bomber crewmen, at least thirty-nine (one in a hundred) were killed in action, while thirty-one were taken prisoner after bailing out and forty-three evaded capture. My tally does not include two P-51 fighter pilots also killed, one whose plane went unaccountably out of control and crashed in the Adriatic, another who simply vanished in a cloud. The figures, too, almost certainly understated the number of casualties, as I had no data on airmen wounded or killed by flak in bombers that returned to base.

I did some simple analysis of the figures and tried to put them in the larger context of the air war. Fourteen bombers out of a total force of 390 worked out to a loss rate of 3.6 percent—well above the 1 percent rate deemed "acceptable" by Air Corps strategists, although less than some other missions. During "Big Week" of February 21, 1944, for example, when the Eighth and Fifteenth Air Forces combined in a coordinated effort to smash German war production, losses averaged 6 percent per mission, with the Fifteenth losing nearly a fifth of its planes in just three missions. On nineteen raids carried out between April and August of the same year against the fiercely defended oil refineries at Ploesti, Romania, the Fifteenth averaged a 4 percent loss per mission. And on the famous low-level attack of August 1, 1943, against Ploesti, losses totaled 33 percent, the worst for any major mission of the war.

Statistics aside, the accounts of screaming metal and of wounded and dying men in the skies over Winterhaven spoke for themselves. Aboard the *Liberty Belle*, the eleventh crewman was luck.

■

The recollections of Rudy and my father and the documentary materials were an encouraging start, but further progress would depend on finding other members of the *Liberty Belle* crew. Besides Rudy, the only other crew member whose whereabouts I knew was Keith Martin, the bombardier. Although my father hadn't seen or spoken to him since 1944, my mother and Martin's wife had kept up the ritual of exchanging Christmas cards. I wrote Martin telling him of my project and what I had learned to date and asking him for his own recollections, but received no immediate reply.

From the *Liberty Belle*'s missing air crew report I had the names and serial numbers of the rest of the crewmen and their home addresses as of 1944. Other than this, I knew nothing about them—no current addresses or, for that matter, who in the crew was still alive. After forty years the trail would be stone cold. Where to begin? A search notice in the newsletter of the Fifteenth Air Force Association, an organization whose membership overwhelmingly comprised veterans of World War II, brought no response. Officials at the Air Force Archives suggested writing county offices of vital records, state adjutant generals and veterans bureaus, and the Military Personnel Records Center in St. Louis. But none of these leads panned out—the information either wasn't available or was protected by privacy laws. The replies from the national headquarters of the American Legion and Veterans of Foreign Wars were polite, but I learned that as a matter of policy, these organizations do not furnish names of members.

Hoping to reach the *Liberty Belle* crewmen directly, I placed classified ads in the newspapers of their home towns as of 1944. A typical notice, this one in the *Essex County Republican*, of Elizabethtown, New York, read:

CORBO, NICHOLAS J., former Withersbee resident, flew in B-24 in WWII—son of fellow crew member is seeking whereabouts. Contact: J. Merritt, 51 N. Main St., Pennington, N.J. 08534 or call collect nights: 609 737-0496.

A month after placing this notice, I received a call from a woman identifying herself as Marie Sherrill of Withersbee. She was Nicholas Corbo's sister. After the war, she recalled, "We'd gotten so much mail from all the crew members. After a while we stopped hearing from them, so it was amazing to see this notice in the paper after all these years!

My pharmacist pointed it out to me. I didn't know what to make of it and called my sister about it. We wondered who you were and why you were trying to reach our brother."

As we talked, it became clear that she had not shared the notice with Nicholas Corbo.

"And your brother," I asked—"he's still living?"

"Very much so," she said, "although he's rather down-hearted about losing his wife last July. He'd just retired after forty years with RCA, and they were planning a trip to Hawaii before she died. It's been hard. They had no children, but he's got four sisters and three brothers, and we've all been looking after him."

Her brother, she added, lived an hour south of her, in Rensselaer, near Albany. She hadn't told him about the notice because she had been waiting to talk to me first.

"I'll be happy to call him if you'd like," she offered.

"That's okay. You've been extremely helpful!"

Immediately after hanging up I dialed her brother's number. A man's voice answered by the third ring.

"Is this Nicholas Corbo?" I asked.

When he replied in the affirmative, I explained who I was and my purpose in calling. For a moment he was speechless. "This is amazing—I can't believe who you are!" Then he asked, "How old are you?"

I laughed. "Forty-one—a lot older than you and my father were when you knew each other."

"Is your dad still alive? And what about your mom? She was a beautiful woman, the last person we saw when we left to go overseas. I'll never forget her there at the railroad station in Riverside."

I assured him that both my mother and dad were alive and well. We talked about other members of the crew. He said that Carver, the tail gunner, had resided in the same area for some years after the war but that he had eventually lost touch with him. "He lived in Hoosick Falls but then moved to Vermont, as I recall—I think to Bennington. Let me see what I can do about finding him."

I referred to the tail gunner as "Harry" Carver, as this was how he had been listed on the missing air crew report. Corbo corrected me, saying that among the crew he was known as Gil.

"When we bailed out," he added, "Gil was a little ahead of the rest of us, which I think is why he got captured."

■

A month later I was on the New York Thruway, driving north from my home in New Jersey to meet Nick Corbo. It was a gray day in early January, a year after I had started the search for my father's wartime past. I had tried to arrange a rendezvous that included my dad, but a combination of circumstances—bad weather, holidays, and a post-Christmas trip to Florida by my parents—conspired against it. Actually, I was just as glad to be making the trip by myself, for I remained doubtful of the project's success and reluctant to involve my father in something whose outcome seemed so problematical. I still needed to locate and interview other members of the crew, wherever they might be. Ultimately, too, my father and I would have to visit Yugoslavia and retrace his route, hoping to find people who had helped him along the way—a prospect that seemed dauntingly remote.

I found Nick Corbo's house, a yellow-shingled bungalow at the top of a winding street in a subdivision of modest homes. He greeted me on the porch, a stocky, smiling man in his early sixties, with dark graying hair, wearing a gray V-neck sweater over a turtleneck. By now, we had spoken enough times on the phone that it seemed like meeting an old friend. In the living room he introduced me to Marie Sherrill and her husband, who had come down for the afternoon from Withersbee.

Gil Carver, the tail gunner, was also there. Nick had managed to find him; he had indeed moved to Vermont some years before but had since returned to Hoosick Falls, New York, less than an hour from Nick's home. A jowly, avuncular figure of medium height, in a plaid wool shirt and with a full, dark head of hair, he rose slowly from his chair and with a bemused smile shook my hand.

How many times over the years, I wondered, had I told people of my father's Yugoslavia experience? The brief recital had always concluded with the line, "He got his crew out okay, except for the tail gunner, who was captured." Now I was face to face with that very tail gunner, a character in a childhood fable come to life.

All of us sat down, and I turned on my tape recorder. For the next hour, Nick and Gil reminisced about their years in the Air Corps and filled me in on their postwar civilian lives. Nick had spent his career as an electrician on the technical staff at the local RCA plant. Gil, who at thirty had been the old man of the crew (a fact I hadn't known before our meeting), was now in his early seventies and had retired some years ago from the U.S. Postal Service. He had two grown sons, one living in Florida and the other, a lawyer, in Bismarck, North Dakota.

Our conversation turned to the Vienna mission and its aftermath. Sitting next to me on the couch, Nick recalled the intense flak over the target and his sense of relief as soon as

Martin released the bombs. "I figured that was it—we made this one. Then I heard this tremendous roar, and we got it. That was the hit that blew out the nose wheel and made a big gaping hole next to the copilot's seat. Then we started losing speed. I couldn't understand why at first, until I realized that flak must have hit the governors on two of the engines because they were running wild. Your dad was having a rough time, and I remember his going into a nose dive to get speed up and keep us from stalling. Somehow we got out of there and were still flying an hour later. It looked for a while that we might have to ditch in the Adriatic, and your dad got on the interphone and asked if everyone could swim. Me and Wheeler both said we couldn't. Then Rudolph reported we were over Partisan territory and your dad gave the order to bail out."

I had questions about the bailout sequence and about the confusion in the back of the plane.

"It was pretty hectic," said Nick, who had been with my dad and Rudy on the flight deck, in the forward part of the airplane. "I don't remember the exact order we jumped, except that Gil was the first one out. Cunningham got on the interphone and said that Wheeler wouldn't jump. Then I heard him say that Wheeler was out and he was going next."

Gil Carver, the "tail gunner, who was captured" of my boyhood stories, smiled at the recollection.

"All I remember was getting out of there fast," he said. "I landed in a tree, and it took me about ten minutes to get free. There was a road, and I saw this guy. I tried to indicate that I was looking for Partisans. He pointed up the road and motioned me to come with him, so we began walking. Before long we ran into this rag-tag group of eight or ten

Yugoslavians. They were wearing a bunch of different uniforms and carrying weapons. I surrendered my forty-five to them—Army intelligence told us to give our guns to the Partisans, and anyway, I figured then and there that, for me, the war was over."

The soldiers informed Carver that he had landed in the "Independent Republic of Hrvatska." They took him to a town and put him up in a hotel for a week. "I felt like some strange animal in a zoo. I couldn't complain, though. They treated me pretty nice, and I ate good—a lot better than in Italy, where the chow was awful. A priest who spoke some English interrogated me. Once he asked me to draw a picture of my plane, and I drew this real fanciful picture of a bomber bristling with guns. I thought that would impress them."

The town had German troops in it. He recalled the Yugoslavs taking him out for a haircut and shunting him into a doorway to avoid some Nazi soldiers seeing him. By now it was obvious that the people holding him weren't Partisans, although he had no idea what faction they represented. One day, the Yugoslavs put him into the back of a truck with some members of a wedding party, including the bride and groom. "We drove out into the country and had a picnic and some drinks. Then they motioned me back on the truck, took me into Zagreb, and turned me over to the Germans."

The Germans locked him up in a prison outside the city. Two other American airmen soon joined him. After several days of interrogation, he was placed on a train to Vienna, where in a kind of cruel poetic justice he sweated out a bombing raid by the Fifteenth Air Force. "Then they sent me to Budapest. I was there about a week, most of the time in solitary because I wouldn't answer their questions. They wanted to know things like who else was in my crew. Finally I made up a list of names, all dead people I had known. That got me out of solitary."

Next stop was a prison camp on the Baltic and internment for the rest of the war. "The camp was divided into separate compounds for American, British, and Russians. The Russians did all the work—the Germans treated them terribly. They hassled us just a little, bringing us out for roll call in the middle of the night, that sort of thing. It wasn't too bad until right near the end of the war, when Russian troops started closing in and we were forced to evacuate. The Germans marched us from one town to another. Conditions were terrible; the roads were filled with refugees and there was hardly any food to go around. A lot of guys got sick, and someone was dying every day. When I finally got home—on May 30, 1945, the day after my wedding anniversary—I weighed ninety-six pounds."

When his wife received the missing-in-action telegram, Gil said, she fainted. For all she knew, he was dead, for it took another three months to learn that he had been taken prisoner.

In Nick Corbo's case, the telegram from the War Department arrived while his family was having Sunday dinner. His mother and father, four sisters, and two younger brothers (a third, older, brother was in the Navy) were seated at the table when the doorbell rang. As Marie Sherrill recalled, "The man who brought the news was a deacon at our church and managed the A&P. Somehow, he'd made a mistake and brought us the wrong telegram—it was for someone *killed* in action. I guess he got ours mixed up with another family's. Anyway, our mother got up from dinner to answer the door. We didn't know who was there at first but realized something was wrong when we heard a thump—she passed out from the news. Then the messenger realized he'd made a mistake. He went back and returned a half-hour later with the right telegram, telling us Nick was missing in action."

I was struck by the dreamlike quality of both Marie's story and Gil's account of his capture. Neither made complete sense, and pressing the tellers failed to clear up inexplicable details. Given the seriousness of the telegram, for example, how could the messenger have made such a mistake? And why did he have to return to the Western Union office to retrieve the right telegram? If the problem was really a mix-up in telegrams, it would be more logical for him to have had both telegrams in his possession and to have handed the wrong one to Nick's mother.

(There was no such confusion when my mother received her missing-in-action telegram. She and I were living with my grandmother in Waco. Mother took the news with her usual calm, then called her younger and more excitable sister. My aunt, who had an equally improbable southern name—Billie Bob—was also married to a pilot. They were living in Fort Worth, about a hundred miles away, and had just returned from a movie. She left for Waco the next morning but was so upset she forgot to check her fuel gauge and ran out of gas en route. Years later she recalled, "A nice man picked me up—they didn't murder you in those days—and took me to Mother's." Later, a friend drove her back to retrieve her car.)

Gil's story was even stranger than Marie's. What faction were the Yugoslavs who had taken him into custody? Why had they hidden him for an entire week, then turned him over to the Germans? The bizarrest touch of all, like something out of an avant garde film, was his joining the wedding picnic, prior to being turned over to the Germans.

During the period their sons were missing, Gil said, several mothers of *Liberty Belle* crewmen exchanged letters, trying to keep up hope. He had brought a letter with him, written on blue air-mail stationery, from Wheeler's mother to his. "She was always quoting from the Bible and must have been real religious. She had two boys in the service besides Robert—one who was shot up in Europe and the other just going in when the war ended."

I asked Nick what his dominant mood had been while in Yugoslavia. Was he afraid, confident about getting home, or what? He reflected a moment before answering. "I was scared 80 percent of the time," he said, leaning forward and clasping his hands. "Looking back on it now, I don't think I should have been, and a lot of the things that scared me were fabricated. For instance, you'd hear shooting and think it was the Germans coming after you, but actually it was just the Partisans celebrating because they'd taken a town or something. We always had a sense of the Germans being close when really they weren't." Nick couldn't recall "ever coming face to face" with the enemy except possibly one time, when he and several other crewmen were standing outside a farmhouse and thought they saw a German on patrol, several hundred yards away. Perhaps it was only in retrospect that they realized this lone figure might be trouble. Anyway, their response was to wave at him. The German soldier, if that's what he was, waved back.

"Artie Dupree was with me most of the time, and he took everything pretty good," Nick added. "Nothing ever scared him, and he calmed me down quite a bit."

On the table in front of me were two faded snapshots
Nick had found. One was taken in September 1944 and
showed him, Dupree, and Wheeler strolling down a street in
Foggia or Naples—three kids in fatigue jackets, overseas
caps tilted jauntily on their heads. The other, taken during
stateside training, showed him, Gil Carver, and Len Cole at
the start of a furlough. They looked neat and fit and forever
young in their ties and starched khaki blouses, grinning
under the California sky, arms on each other's shoulders:
buddies.

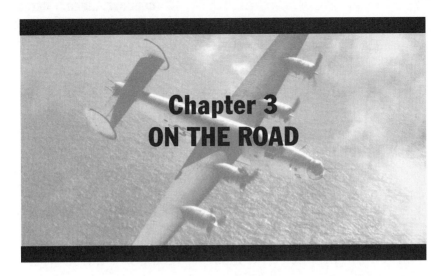

Chapter 3
ON THE ROAD

Exhausted from the day's ordeal, the *Liberty Belle* crewmen fell fast asleep within an hour of nightfall. Less than twenty-four hours before, they had been secure in the relative comfort of their squadron tents at San Giovanni. Now their bed was dank straw spread on the dirt floor of a barn, somewhere in the northern Yugoslavian republic of Croatia.

It seemed that they had barely closed their eyes when their sleep was interrupted by a Partisan shaking them awake. In his excited speech they recognized only one word: "*Germanski*!"

Johnson glanced at his watch: the luminous dial read three o'clock. He tightened the laces of his G.I. shoes and with the others followed the Partisan out of the barn and into the misty night.

The trail took them single file up and down hills, through woods, and along the edge of fields. They were on the move for two hours before dawn broke, when they stopped to rest. The Partisan knew a little English, enough to make them understand that the Germans had learned of their hiding place and had sent a patrol to find them.

Following several more hours of walking, they reached

another village, this one bigger than yesterday's, extending a quarter mile on either side of a dirt road. A woman fixed them some milk broth, and as they drank it eagerly a crowd gathered around to watch. Already they were getting used to their strange celebrity status.

A local Partisan named Magdic spoke excellent English. He took them on a tour of the village, which he identified as Topolovac. It had been attacked by German planes several months before, he said. Some of the homes had been completely destroyed, while others stood roofless and pockmarked by shrapnel. A woman pointed out a house where some of her relatives had been killed. Making the most of this propaganda opportunity, Magdic impressed on the Americans the enemy's ruthlessness, pointing out a cellar in which he claimed children had been killed, and the remains of a Serbian Orthodox church plundered by the Ustashi, the fascists who controlled Croatia.

The church's blackened stones and bombed-out windows were mute testimony to ethnic rivalries as indigenous to Yugoslavia as the rough beauty of its landscape. The *Liberty Belle* crewmen were but dimly aware of the political and military situation in which they found themselves. Essentially, they had fallen into an occupied country engaged in a three-way civil war, one that would ultimately claim the lives of 1.7 million Yugoslavians, or more than one in ten of the population. (Of all the nations caught up in World War II, only Russia and Poland would lose a higher percentage of their people.) The immediate causes of this war-within-a-war could be traced to the flawed founding of modern Yugoslavia—the name means country of the "South Slavs"—following World War I, when the Allies had stitched together a region of two alphabets, three religions, four languages, and five nationalities into a single Balkan state under a constitutional monarchy.

Rent by internal strife, mainly between the two most populous groups, the Serbs and Croats, this fragile union was torn apart by the geopolitical forces loosed by World War II. In April 1941, German and Italian troops poured into Yugoslavia. Hitler's motivation for attacking the Balkans was securing his southern flank in preparation for the invasion of Russia, which followed in June. Mussolini's was simple territorial greed. The Axis invasion crushed the regular forces of Yugoslavia's young King Peter, who fled to England to set up a government in exile. It also provoked armed resistance by two guerrilla groups, the Chetniks and the Partisans. Led by a former army officer named Drazha Mihailovic, the Chetniks were royalists and mainly Serbian. The Partisans were commanded by Josip Broz Tito, an iron-willed Communist who would emerge as the postwar leader of a socialist, nonaligned Yugoslavia.

Although Chetniks and Partisans looked on each other as the primary enemy, early in the war they occasionally joined forces to fight the occupying Germans. At other times, Chetniks joined with Italians and Germans in fighting the Partisans. Such shifting alliances were not limited to the Yugoslav factions. In the first two years of the Balkan campaign, Italian units allied with the Germans fought alongside Chetniks against the Partisans; after Italy's capitulation, in 1943, many of these same Italian troops went over to the Partisans to fight Germans and Chetniks. The Chetnik commander, Mihailovic, regarded his accommodation with Axis troops as "parallel action" rather than true collaboration, and in temporarily siding with the invaders to further his own political ends he was following an ancient Balkan strategy known as "the uses of the enemy." The Partisans were not persuaded by this historical precedent, however, and after the war they executed Mihailovic as a collaborator.

If anything, the situation in Croatia was even more complex. In the Axis dismemberment of Yugoslavia, Croatia became an independent state under the control of the fiercely nationalistic Ustashi (roughly translated, the name means "the risen") and its leader, Ante Pavelic, a Nazi fellow-traveler who invoked a home-grown version of the Final Solution against "aliens" within his territory: Jews, Gypsies, and Serbs. In a kind of genocidal triage, Pavelic declared that a third of all Serbs residing in Croatia and neighboring Bosnia would be expelled, a third converted to Catholicism from their native Serbian Orthodox, and a third exterminated.

An Italian journalist reported that Pavelic kept at his desk a basket brimming with the eyeballs of Ustashi victims. Even the Germans were appalled by the zeal of the Ustashi in carrying out their pogroms. The Partisans repeatedly told the *Liberty Belle* crewmen how fortunate they were that only one of them (Carver, the tail gunner) had fallen into the hands of the enemy. They did not realize, of course, that Carver at that very moment was being held in relative luxury by Ustashi auxiliaries, the Croatian Home Guard, who would keep him in custody for nearly a week before turning him over to the Germans. The delay suggests the ambivalence the Ustashi themselves may have felt about collaborating with the invaders.

Carver was still on the minds of his fellow crewmen as they toured the ruined village, and they could only hope that he had somehow survived. Except for a few minor injuries— Johnson's sprained back and the cut on Wheeler's hand—

they were all healthy. What's more, according to their interpreter, Magdic, they might soon be on their way home.
Three days' march from here, he promised, was an airfield
where they could expect a plane to fly them back to Italy.

The Partisans were pleased to have the Americans in
their charge; the airmen were a link to the outside world, a
tangible reminder that Yugoslavia's fight for the freedom
was part of a larger global effort to destroy fascism. Rein-
forcing this notion was Partisan propaganda dispersed at
local political congresses during breaks in the fighting. It
happened that one such gathering was going on right now a
few kilometers from the village, and Magdic insisted that
the airmen attend it. Most of them wanted only to sleep, so
Merritt begged off but agreed to send two representatives.
To decide on the honor, they drew straws.

Johnson and Cunningham came up short in the draw and
reluctantly set off with Magdic. When they arrived at the
congress, they found that it had more the air of a picnic than
a serious political meeting. A few tables and benches were
set up with food and drink. As usual, the Americans became
the instant focus of attention. Magdic and a Partisan photographer, Tomo Blazic, took pictures of the two airmen surrounded by a curious and admiring throng. Although the
crowd included several young women, most of the participants were older men in disheveled clothes and short-peaked
caps, looking like steerage class at Ellis Island. The airmen
sat at a table—the dark-haired, stocky Cunningham in flight
coveralls and a bemused grin, Johnson in an overseas cap
and khaki shirt with sergeant's stripes, lean and tall and
quintessentially American. Magdic interpreted the words of
welcome and the Partisan speeches. Johnson reciprocated by
emphasizing the importance of the Partisans' struggle

against the Nazis and their help in rescuing Allied airmen. "We are proud of the fight you are carrying on—Viva Yugoslavia!"

■

My information on the Partisan congress came directly from Art Johnson, whom I met in March 1986, several months after he had called me from his home in Fair Oaks, California (north of San Francisco), in response to one of my personal ads seeking the *Liberty Belle* crewmen. The ad had appeared in the *Journal-Advocate* of Sterling, Colorado, his home of record during the war. Although he had not lived in Sterling since 1942, his brother was still there and had spotted the ad. Art told me over the phone that he had recently retired after forty years of teaching in public and private schools, and that, with time on his hands, he had begun thinking about his wartime experiences for the first time in decades. He spoke in a soft, friendly, western voice. "I wanted to see about trying to get back in touch with my old crewmates—your notice in the paper was a miracle."

He reminisced for several minutes about his tour with the Fifteenth Air Force and his fate to have been assigned to the *Liberty Belle* as a substitute gunner. I learned of the thirty missions he had flown with his original crew and of his medical grounding and assignment to temporary duty as a clerk, a job that included filling out missing-in-action reports for crews that didn't return. "There was a lot of joking about this when I got ready to go back on flight duty. Before leaving on the Vienna mission with your dad, I told the first sergeant, 'If we get shot down, maybe I'll be able to write up my own missing-in-action report when we get back.'"

Art said he would send me some photographs and an account, written shortly after the war, of the *Liberty Belle*'s last mission and his experiences in Yugoslavia. We talked about the possibility of getting together, perhaps with bombardier Keith Martin, who lived in southern California. When I mentioned that Maes and Wheeler had originally been from California, he volunteered to try tracking them down: "I know a person in the state motor vehicle agency who might be able to help."

A month later, Art called back to tell me that he had struck paydirt. Maes, he learned, lived just a couple of hours west of him, in Healdsburg. Wheeler turned out to be even closer; Art was surprised to discover that he lived in the neighboring town of Carmichael and that his house was only about eight blocks away. After speaking to Wheeler on the phone, he said, they had visited briefly. "When I called him up he only vaguely remembered me at first. We've lived this close to each other for the last six years and have probably been within shouting distance plenty of times, but after forty years I don't think we would have recognized each other."

With Art Johnson's help I had now located eight of the ten *Liberty Belle* crewmen. In the course of my research I would also find members of several other crews who had been with my dad's in Yugoslavia and whose recollections would add important details to the story. I had less success with the remaining two *Liberty Belle* crewmen, however. Correspondence with the veterans agencies of Minnesota and Mississippi turned up tantalizing evidence that Elliott Cunningham and Arnold Dupree were still alive, although no longer resident in their home states, and that they were probably aware I was looking for them. But either out of indifference or for personal reasons which I had no choice but to respect, they never came forward.

■

Fourteen months after beginning the search for my father's past, I flew out to the West Coast to meet with the California contingent of the *Liberty Belle* crew. Accompanying me was my sixteen-year-old daughter, Jennifer. In part I brought her along because she wanted to look at some West Coast colleges, and it was convenient to combine our purposes in a single trip. I was also interested in her perspectives on the people we would meet and wanted to involve her in exploring her grandfather's role in one of history's epic events.

The California spring was a revelation. Refugees from the gray New Jersey winter, we drove north from San Francisco, astonished by the roadside flowers and emerald hillsides dotted with live oaks. We spent the night in Sacramento and the next morning drove to Fair Oaks to meet Art and Polly Johnson at their suburban ranch house. A stylized fish, symbol of the Christian church, graced their front door. Art looked vigorous and fit at age sixty-two, a big man with a soft voice and blue eyes that crinkled when he smiled. I sensed his strength and underlying seriousness, qualities my father had noted early in their Yugoslavia experience. The living-room wall hung with portraits of his pioneer family. His parents had homesteaded a 160-acre farm on the Colorado prairie, he told me, and had instilled in their son a firm religious faith.

"Everyone in the family calls him the preacher," said Polly.

Of his postwar career, Art said, "I got out of the service

on a Friday and was enrolled the following Monday at Pasadena Nazarene College. I got my teaching credentials at U.S.C., taught five years at a private military academy, then spent thirty years in the public schools as a teacher and administrator. The last five years, until my retirement last June, was in a private school run by our church."

Robert Wheeler came over from his home in Carmichael. When I had spoken to him on the phone a month earlier, he had shown little enthusiasm for my project. "I'm happy to talk to you, but only so long as you don't write anything that glorifies us," he insisted. "We were just a bunch of kids in a situation we didn't comprehend. None of us did anything heroic." Yet he was friendly enough when we met and irrepressible once he got going. A wiry, alert man of medium height, he told us about his boyhood in Yucaipa (yu-KY-pa," he said, correcting my pronunciation) and the consuming interest in electronics that had started him on his magical mystery tour of duty assignments—radar and radio schools, O.S.S. training, gunnery school, night-fighter training, B-24 submarine patrol, and finally posting to my father's crew at March Field.

After the war, he studied engineering and went into defense work for Sherman Fairchild, on Long Island. He was involved in missile design, conceptual work on an atomic aircraft engine, and developing instruments for the first unmanned moon shot. The work was exciting but stressful; beset by ulcers, he abandoned his high-tech career in the early 1970s and returned to California to grow pears on a farm inherited by his wife.

As we sat at the dining room table listening to Robert talk, I imagined what he might have been like as a kid. If born forty years later, he would have been a computer jock. My neat-to-a-fault father remembered him as a brilliant radioman, able to fix any piece of electronics, and also as the scruffiest member of the crew. As for Robert's perspective on my father: "Your dad ran a tight crew, which wasn't always the case in the Air Corps, and he made sure that everyone was qualified at their jobs. He was kind of standoffish and discouraged fraternization between officers and men. That didn't bother me at all; I applauded it."

About the Vienna mission and bailing out, he recalled, "After we were hit over the target, your dad called on the intercom to say he couldn't get any response out of the 522—that was the radio we used to communicate with fighters. I had to get off the intercom and climb up to where the 522 was located, in the radio equipment area above the wing root. I knew we were going to have to bail out, so I took off my electric flying suit and muckaluks, changed into my G.I. shoes, and went up there to check out the radio. I'd never flown in this version of a B-24 and couldn't find the 522 at all. At first I thought maybe it was just in a different part of the plane; then I realized it had been blown away by flak."

With the radio gone, Wheeler crawled back to his post in the rear of the plane. "By now your dad had told everybody to bail out, but I never got the message. It seemed like just a matter of minutes since we got hit, and I assumed we were still over Austria, until I looked out the window and saw mountains at our level. Finally I figured out what was happening. Everybody seemed to be standing around the camera hatch. They all looked scared to death and no one was moving. I thought I would do something and got down on my hands and knees next to the hatch."

Robert stopped at this point in the story and jumped out of his chair to demonstrate how, forty-two years before, he had crouched down in the rear of the bomber. "It was a real awkward position, and the hatch seemed barely big enough to get your head through. I was trying to remember what they'd taught us about bailing out—I didn't want to roll and start spinning. I guess there must have been some hesitation on my part, because the next thing I knew, someone had stuck his boot in my butt and kicked me out. I was mad as hell and swearing at the so-and-so all the way down."

"You were just being . . . deliberate," I said.

Art smiled, and Robert turned to him. "I never realized it until this guy got together with me a few weeks ago, but *he* was the son-of-a-gun who booted me out of the plane."

When I asked about their state of mind while in Yugoslavia, Robert said that he had never worried except once, when Art came down with flu and had to be strapped to a horse while they moved between towns. "He was almost in a coma on that horse. It was raining like crazy, and he had a high fever—put your hand on him and he was burning. It was pitch dark, there was cold rain and snow and he kept sliding off the horse. You'd see him upright for a minute and then someone would call 'He's down!', and we'd push him back up."

He remembered that some of them assumed—wrongly— that next-of-kin had been notified about their being safely in Partisan hands. Although a British liaison officer radioed their names to the Fifteenth Air Force's headquarters, in Bari, for reasons having to do with either security or bureaucratic inertia, the information went no further—not even to group headquarters. Art remembered the friend to whom he'd given his diaries turning "ashen white" when he walked into the room after returning to Italy. "Someone had reported our plane going down with no parachutes, so he never expected to see me again."

Robert recalled repairing Partisan radios and listening to

German propaganda broadcasts by the British traitor Axis Sally. "She'd be saying 'Hello you boys of the 455th' and that sort of thing—she always knew when a plane had crashed, where it had gone down, and the names of the crew members. Everyone seemed to know we were alive except the folks back home."

One of those kept in the dark about their loved ones was Polly Johnson. She and Art had met in college and became engaged before he went overseas. "I'd finished school and was working for a doctor in Pasadena," she said. "When Art was shot down I didn't find out at first, but I had a premonition that something was wrong. I'd received letters from him every day and then the letters stopped. When his mother in Colorado got the telegram from the War Department, she wired me with the news."

After returning to the States, Art made a beeline to Pasadena as soon as he was granted leave. "I got into town at 10 A.M. and we were married at eight o'clock that night."

"He got in that morning, and we went to the lab right away for a blood test—the doctor I worked for had made the arrangements," said Polly. "My friends asked me, 'You haven't seen him in two years and you're going to marry him? You're not worried?' We'd all heard stories about men coming back changed by the war, but I knew him and wasn't concerned. There were six hundred people at our wedding that night, and an audible gasp went up from the congregation when Art appeared. He'd lost thirty-five pounds in Yugoslavia and everyone assumed he'd be emaciated, but he'd gained it all back by then and looked fine."

Art interjected: "When our troop ship got into New York they sent us to Camp Shanks on the Hudson for processing. When I sat down for my first meal there I ate two steaks and drank two quarts of milk."

"The only way you could tell he'd been affected by his experience in Yugoslavia was on our honeymoon," Polly said. "If I was across the room and he was asleep, I'd have to call to wake him up before getting into bed—otherwise he'd react. That was the only thing I ever noticed, and of course it went away after a while."

Before we left, Art remembered an item he wanted to show me. He disappeared for a minute and returned with a walking stick. He had injured his back in parachuting, he said, and had carried the stick throughout Yugoslavia. A long row of notches ran up its polished flank—forty-nine in all, one for each day of their exodus.

■

We found Don Maes and his wife, Arline, living on the top of a hill near Healdsburg, deep in the wine country of Sonoma County. A sign over the gateway of the dirt road leading to their house read "El Rancho de Ardon." ("Ardon" being a contraction, he explained, of their two first names.) Other ranch houses, some with backyard vineyards, were perched on neighboring hills dotted with cattle and live oak. The house was warm, expansive, and archetypically Californian, complete with a redwood deck and outdoor Jacuzzi.

Don told me proudly that he had built most of the house with his own hands, working from a design found in a magazine and with help from his three sons (two were general contractors and one was a doctor). Tanned and robust, with full hair, thick arms, and barrel chest, he had spent most of his life outdoors. The son of Belgium immigrants, he had grown up in Huntington Beach and El Monte, near Los Angeles. "As kids we used to hitch-hike to the beach every day to go body-surfing. It was a typical southern California upbringing, and I've got the skin cancer spots to show for it." After the war, he and his brother-in-law went into truck farming, a business that proved successful enough for him to retire at age fifty and move to June Lake, in the Sierra Nevada, where he operated a ski lift for ten years before settling in Healdsburg to be near their physician son and his family.

As the *Liberty Belle*'s copilot, Don was another character in the saga I had known since childhood. Whenever my father talked of the Vienna mission, he invariably mentioned that a piece of flak had burst through the flight deck and gone out the top of the cockpit, passing within inches of the copilot's legs. As the story went, the copilot wasn't flying the plane at the moment, so that his legs were tucked beneath him rather than extended to the rudder pedals; otherwise, his legs would have been blown away.

"Actually," said Don, "I don't remember if my legs were extended or not, and I think the shrapnel came up between us, just to the left of my knee." Vienna, he added, "was always really bad for flak, and on that mission the stuff was close enough for us to hear it exploding and see the red flash in the center. Somewhere around here I've got some souvenir pieces, bits of shrapnel I'd find in the plane after a mission."

He took Jennifer and me into his study to show us some war memorabilia, first pointing out a picture of his seven grandchildren (arrayed according to size) and other shots of the Maes clan skiing and rafting in the Sierra Nevada. The materials included a pastel sketch of Don by a Partisan artist as well as the missing-in-action telegram and other official correspondence to Arline. A letter from the commanding general of the Fifteenth Air Force struck me as a model of obfuscating boilerplate:

31 October 1944

Dear Mrs. Maes:

I wish I could give you some assurance of the safety of your husband, Second Lieutenant Donald V. Maes, o-713522, who has been missing in action since October 7, 1944, when he failed to return from an operational flight to Vienna, Austria, but the facts available are too indefinite for the basis of an opinion.

Over the target his ship left the formation and continued to fall behind the group. As heavy flak was encountered the attention of the others was diverted to flying. I hope that the men reached the earth safely. I can do little but assure you that the War Department will notify you should further information be received in the future.

I am proud to have had your husband in my command. It is inspiring to know that men of his courage and ability are carrying on our nation's battles against the aggressor. In recognition of meritorious achievement he has been awarded the Air Medal.

Very sincerely yours,
N. F. TWINING
Major General, USA
Commanding

While in Yugoslavia, said Don, "I was more worried about the people at home than about myself. Arline was pregnant at the time with Bruce, our oldest son. I had written my brother-in-law saying that if anything happened to me, they shouldn't worry, because I might have been taken prisoner or survived in some other way, even if they didn't hear anything. He kept the letter like I asked and read it to Arline after I was reported missing."

He opened a scrapbook containing snapshots of the crew taken in Bari within a few days after their return to Italy. There was a group shot of them standing in a semi-circle in front of the squadron orderly shack—at ease, hands in pockets, secure in the knowledge that they would soon be going home.

My eye scanned the individual shots and stopped on the picture of my dad. At the time it was taken he would have been closer to Jennifer's age than my own, and with his tousled hair and lean frame he looked barely out of adolescence. I studied the photo as he smiled self-consciously at me across four decades. His left hand was bandaged (the result of a cut and subsequent infection while in Yugoslavia), and the fatigue sweater pulled tight over his blouse was easily three sizes too small. (Wardrobes for repatriated airmen were catch-as-catch-can, their regular clothes having been shipped home.) Otherwise, he appeared fit and not even especially thin, although he had lost thirty-five pounds.

"See this one?" I said to Jennifer. "That's your grandfather."

She gasped. "That's Poppy? He was so young!"

■

Once Johnson and Cunningham returned from the Partisan congress, the *Liberty Belle* crewmen were on their way again, trudging south to Roviice, a village about four miles away, where they joined a convoy of wagons carrying clothes and other Partisan supplies. It had been overcast all afternoon, and as the convoy pulled out at dark it began raining hard. The downpour continued for the next four hours, turning the road into a quagmire. Pulled by emaciated horses, the wagons slipped and slid through the ankle-deep mud.

The night was black and the terrain even rougher than before—they could barely see their hands in front of their faces, and some of the steeper hills were negotiated on hands and knees. Soaked to the skin and bone-tired, they staggered to the outskirts of the village of St. Ivan Zabno, where a peasant woman gave them some bread and hot soup and the floor of her cottage to rest. They were just dozing off when the Partisan hustled them to their feet and out the door. It looked like another night on the run, but the Partisan only took them as far as the summit of a nearby hill.

The rain had stopped, and the sky had even begun to clear a bit. The moon sailed through roiling clouds, and in the silver light they had a broad view of the valley. The caravan had gone on without them, the Partisans thinking it better for the airmen to avoid the village, where Ustashi spies might be lurking. After a couple of hours on the hill, their escort rallied them again; cutting overland, they were reunited with the wagons beyond St. Ivan Zabno.

It was now early in the morning of Monday, October 9, the beginning of their second full day in Yugoslavia. They were cold, wet, and hungry, and the rain started again as the caravan got underway. At noon they stopped at another village, Srp. Kapela, for a two-hour rest and a lunch of apples and black bread. By mid-afternoon they were on the road again. Except for a pause just before dark, they traveled straight through the night and into the following morning, alternately walking beside the wagons or swaying and bumping inside them in a futile effort to grab a few minutes' sleep.

Their spirits quickened when the Partisans told them that

the airfield was just a few kilometers away—in a matter of hours they could expect to be on a transport flying out of this miserable country! It was six in the morning, and the horizon was beginning to lighten when they heard, coming from beyond the next hill, the rattle of automatic weapons, and saw tracers arcing over the horizon.

The Ustashi were attacking the airfield! There would be no planes landing there this morning. They beat a hasty retreat back to the last village, where the Partisans deliberated for an hour before moving out again, cutting a wide detour around the fighting. The airmen could still hear occasional bursts of gunfire, but the action was mostly over. The Ustashi had taken the airfield, and with it any immediate hope for evacuation.

■

More than anything else about their seven weeks in Yugoslavia, Keith Martin remembered the walking. On forced marches like the one to the airfield, he said, "We'd go twenty or thirty hours without stopping. It was amazing how you could keep it up all day and night on nothing but apples. Sometimes we'd carry a loaf of this horrible black bread to munch on, and we had water. I think you could walk all the way from Los Angeles to New York if someone gave you food and water. You just plod on like a zombie."

He told me this as we sat on the veranda of his house, near Pasadena, on the last leg of my California trip. When I had first written to the *Liberty Belle*'s bombardier nearly a year before my visit, he hadn't responded—this despite a letter of introduction from my father explaining my purpose and alerting him that I would be in touch. A second letter from me, written six months after the first, brought only silence, too. A month before leaving for California, I called his home in hopes of setting up an interview, but learned from his son that he was out of town. Finally, I heard from him indirectly when his wife wrote, inviting us to stay with them when we reached Los Angeles. "I intended to write weeks ago," she said in her note. "Of course, Keith is the one who should be writing to you, but writing letters is not his forte."

His long silence notwithstanding, I liked Keith Martin from the instant he answered the door, and any concerns I may have had about his willingness to talk slipped away as gently as the evening, as we sat on the veranda, sipping bourbon and watching the night fall over the Los Angeles basin. He wore a flowered shirt, open at the collar and with the tails out. His dark, wavy hair and prominent nose reminded me of Richard Nixon, an impression redeemed at once by his droll humor and our common interest in science. He worked as an engineer at the Jet Propulsion Laboratory at the nearby California Institute of Technology, designing tests for the delicate instruments used in NASA space probes. The lack of a college degree (he attended the University of Southern California and Pasadena City College after the war but never graduated) had not deterred him from a successful career. Self-taught in computers, he had written the database software used for testing instruments to be flown aboard the Hubble Space Telescope. "I've got a mind like a sponge," he said. "I can take a manual on how to do something and learn it all in no time."

Keith Martin enjoyed the Jet Propulsion Lab's unstructured nature and thrived in an environment that let him pursue his interests without a lot of oversight. There was still something about him of the rebellious kid who had chafed under Army regulations and who, forty years later, could still complain about the requirement to wear a tie while overseas. (Gil Carver, ten years his senior, had thought him "a little bit crazy." Once on a training flight, he recalled, Martin had taken the controls for some "stick time" and nearly stalled out the plane. On another training flight, he said, Martin had manned the tail turret—normally Carver's post—for a practice strafing run, and in an excess of enthusiasm fired overly long bursts that burned out the barrels of the twin machine guns.)

Our conversation skipped across a range of topics that included his family, the Vienna mission, bailing out, daily life in Yugoslavia and Italy, and his last nine months in the service following repatriation. The son of an accountant, Keith was an only child. He had been born in downtown Los Angeles—"They're not many people who can say that anymore"—and, except for the war years, had spent his entire life in the L.A. area. He and his wife, Betty, met well after the war and were married in 1954. They had two grown children, a son in his mid-twenties living at home and a daughter in an executive position in the Los Angeles office of an international accounting firm.

He recalled in detail the return to the States from Italy. The War Department had decreed that any flier downed in enemy territory and later rescued would be shipped home if he had spent at least forty-two days in-country. This rather arbitrary cutoff was based on the notion that anyone behind enemy lines more than six weeks might no longer be regarded as a regular soldier, and therefore subject to Geneva Convention protocols, but as an irregular—a spy or covert operator, whom the enemy had no scruples about shooting. With forty-nine days in Yugoslavia, the *Liberty Belle* crewmen were comfortably past the magic number.

Following the return to Italy and their debriefing, the *Liberty Belle* crewmen were cut orders shipping them home from Naples on December 10. "We went back on a new troop ship, a huge thing nine hundred feet long," Keith recalled. "There were over seven hundred of us on board. The state rooms where officers normally bunked were filled with hospital cases, so we were stuck down in the hold with the enlisted men. We slept in vertical racks of seven cots each with maybe a foot and a half between them, just enough space to crawl in. It took eleven days coming back, with horrendous storms the whole way. Some of those waves were thirty feet high, and you'd lie in your bunk with the ship crawling along at one or two knots and feel them hit—*wham*! The ship would shudder, then the propellers would come out of the water and the whole thing would start vibrating. They only let us out on deck one or two times the entire trip. We'd eat standing up at this counter about a foot and a half wide running along one side of a passageway. At least once a day, I swear, they served us canned franks and beans. You'd be standing there eating and guys would be throwing up all around you."

At other times, he added, "I'd just sit there smoking a cigar, seeing how long I could hold the ash before tapping it in this peanut can. How's that for desperate entertainment?"

Once back in the states, none of the crew went overseas again. Keith wound up as a physical training officer at Lowry Field, near Denver. "I was smart enough to realize that the top sergeant there was really the one in charge. I showed up once or twice a week and spent the rest of the time riding horseback in the mountains." Don Maes ferried

aircraft around the country. Nick Corbo was posted to
Chenault Field, near Chicago, teaching about electrical systems. My father finished the war as a flight instructor in
Texas. Art Johnson was sent to Alamogordo, New Mexico,
as an electrical specialist on B-29s; when the first atomic
bomb was secretly exploded there, he recalled, it was
reported that an ammo dump had blown up. In California,
Robert Wheeler was assigned to a "special" B-29 crew composed entirely of combat veterans; he had orders to the
Pacific when the war ended, and although he never knew for
sure, he assumed that "special" meant qualified for A-bomb
missions.

Looking back on Yugoslavia, Keith remembered feeling
tired, hungry, and bored, although seldom frightened. He
daydreamed constantly—not about sex (like the others, he
was too exhausted and ill-nourished for that) but about
sugar. Except for the candy bars that arrived in the occasional airdrop, he said, "there was zero sugar in all of
Yugoslavia. Whenever we'd get around to talking about
what we were going to eat when we got back it was always
banana splits, ice cream sundaes, and things like that. Sometimes we'd stop at a farmhouse, and the owner would welcome us by breaking out a bottle of jam. It never had any
sugar in it, though, just blackberries. We'd be so disap-
pointed."

On the home front, Keith's mother prayed for him and,
along with his father, never gave up hope about seeing him
again. In an incident eerily similar to my grandmother's, he
recalled his father having a premonition one night that he
was safe.

"The next day the telegram came, saying I was okay."

Jim Merritt during bomber training, 1944.

*The author's parents in
1943 and 1944.*

"Crew of the Week," as reported in the March Field Beacon.

Airmen Nick Corbo, Len Cole, and Gil Carver at
March Field, California.

Liberty Belle *crewmen Artie Dupree, Nick Corbo, and Robert Wheeler on furlough in Naples or Foggia, September 1944.*

Merritt during debriefing in Italy, several days after his return from Yugoslavia.

The Liberty Belle *crewmen after their return to Italy.*

Clockwise from above: *Crewmen Elliott Cunningham, Artie Dupree, and Carl Rudolph.*

Clockwise from above:
*Crewmen Don Maes, Nick
Corbo, and Art Johnson.*

Elliott Cunningham and Art Johnson at the Partisan congress.

Zarko Gudek, one of the crew's rescuers, posing with a captured German Schmeisser assault rifle.

Dr. Vjenceslav Chytil's house, in Duprava, Croatia, where Merritt and Rudolph enjoyed a dinner and hot bath.

Janez Zerovc, Edi Selhaus, Zarko Gudek, and Jim Merritt during the author and his father's visit to Croatia in September 1986.

Another confab over rakija *and coffee.*

*An old woman recalled the crewmen spending
their first night in Vrhovac.*

Outside the farmhouse where the crew spent its first night in Croatia.

Selhaus gets the lay of the land from residents of Vrhovac.

Merritt examines parts of the Liberty Belle *salvaged from the crash.*

A typical roadside parley. Merritt waits at far right.

Branko Herak with Merritt and Selhaus at the site of the Liberty Belle's *crash forty-two years earlier.*

*Zerovc, the author, and his father listen to Herak describe
the fiery end of the* Liberty Belle.

Chapter 4
THE RETURN

By April 1986, sixteen months after my casual inquiry on New Year's Eve had launched me on my quest, I had learned more than I might ever have hoped about my father's last mission and his escape through Yugoslavia. I had enough information from documents and interviews to fill forty single-spaced pages of a computer file and had collected a drawer full of manila folders crammed with notes and research materials. I had begun studying Serbo-Croatian with a primer and audiocassettes, for I still imagined myself visiting Yugoslavia with my father and any of the *Liberty Belle* crewmen who might wish to join us.

The idea might have seemed hopelessly unrealistic except for some encouraging correspondence of the previous fall. About the same time that I was making initial contact with his old crew members, my father sent me an item from a veteran's magazine that a friend had spotted in a dentist's waiting room. The one-column article was headlined "Slovenians Seek Rescued Airmen" and mentioned a certain John Hribar, of North Point, Florida, who was trying to reunite former Slovenian Partisans with downed American fliers they had helped to rescue during World War II.

Slovenia at the time was the northernmost Yugoslav republic. Although the *Liberty Belle* had gone down in the neighboring republic of Croatia, perhaps Hribar could still be of help in finding Partisans who had assisted my dad and his crew in their escape. Within a week of writing him, I received a reply with the names and addresses of two people to contact: a "Partisan historian" named Edi Selhaus, in Ljubljana, the capital city of Slovenia, and a Janez Zerovc in neighboring Kranj. The note indicated that Zerovc was part of "a group of five people" calling themselves "the Liberator Club."

I wrote Selhaus and Zerovc outlining my project, listing the names of the *Liberty Belle* crewmen and the towns they had passed through, and mentioning the possibility of my father and I visiting Yugoslavia to retrace his steps and to seek out any surviving Partisans who had assisted him.

A few weeks later I heard from both. Zerovc's letter, which arrived first, covered two pages in neat longhand. Although his English was a bit fractured, it was easy enough to get his drift. I was surprised to learn that he and Selhaus had recently completed a book on the rescue of Allied airmen by Slovenians. He was an amateur pilot, he told me, and with Selhaus shared an interest in reuniting American airmen with those who had assisted in their escape. Selhaus, he added, had recently been in touch with the newspaper in Koprivnica "about your matter trying to find the people who remember this event." He promised to write again as soon as they had more news.

Selhaus's letter arrived a few days later. The writing was bigger and less legible than Zerovc's. The script sprawled across the page, with some of the words printed randomly in block letters. In contrast to Zerovc's reserved and businesslike tone, Selhaus's letter exploded with a pell-mell enthusiasm.

                              DECEMBER 11/12/1985
DEAR MR. MERRITT,
thank you very much for your intersting letter! this matter
is the same for you and me namely I am going to write the
second book about allied airman that would be interesting
to me from you THE whole story about how did your
father spent those 49 days among partisans. If you come to
Yugoslavia I'd LIKE to help you very much to find the way,
which your father shall remembers. I'm going now to
writte to the local paper in koprivnica traying to locate the
men who remember . . .
     About all news I'll get, I inform you surelly.
     I wish you and your family Merry Christmas and very
happy NEW YEAR
                              Sincerely
                              Edi Selhaus

Over the winter I wrote Selhaus and Zerovc several more
times, sending them typescript copies of the notes I made
from interviews with the *Liberty Belle* crewmen, at least one
of whom (Don Maes) had expressed some interest in
returning to Yugoslavia. Exploring the possibilities of a
group trip, I made preliminary contact with Pan American
Airways; the airline's director of East European sales turned
out to be a native Yugoslavian, Ivan Dezelic. He put me in
touch with the sales manager of the Hotel Inter-Continental
in Zagreb, who said he could provide an interpreter as well
as accommodations for a group.

With Selhaus and Zerovc helping me, the idea of finding

some of my father's rescuers seemed miraculously in reach. I was fascinated, too, with the possibility of locating the site where the *Liberty Belle* had crashed and recovering some pieces of it, assuming any remained. When I mentioned this to my dad, however, he was doubtful.

"I don't see how we could ever find it," he said. "We crashed in a heavily wooded area and had only the foggiest idea where we were, and we were too busy getting the hell out of there to find out." I knew from the debriefing reports that the plane had gone down about ten kilometers west of Koprivnica. According to the map, there were several villages in the area; perhaps we could find some older residents who could guide us to the site.

The prospect of finding witnesses and visiting the site excited me, but as the months went by and winter merged into spring, I heard nothing more from Selhaus or Zerovc and assumed their efforts had fizzled. Their lack of immediate success left me discouraged; the more I thought about going to Yugoslavia with members of the *Liberty Belle* crew, the more quixotic the idea seemed. The logistics of organizing such a trip aside, I realized that I didn't want the responsibility of being a tour guide in a country I had never set foot in. And it was preposterous to think about going there with a group without some prearranged meeting with the crew's Partisan rescuers, whom Selhaus and Zerovc were apparently having trouble finding.

I thought briefly of going with just my father to explore the territory on our own. Although he expressed a willingness to do so, the notion left me uneasy, to say the least. What if we went there and found—nothing? Like Robert Wheeler kneeling over the camera hatch in the back of the plane, I wasn't at all sure what I was doing.

Against my will, this Yugoslavia business was forcing me to confront some personal matters that I would just as soon avoid. I began to see that the relationship between me and my father had been frozen since I was an adolescent. In his presence I was an eternal sixteen-year-old. Our personalities and interests were so different, and I felt mildly embarrassed and more than a little guilty about it. But that was my problem, not his. When I was growing up, he'd always been reasonable and caring, even if I didn't always appreciate it at the time. In recent years he had become the biggest booster of my writing career, and I was pleased and touched by the obvious pride he took in the one book I had written. He had become its tireless promoter, buying copies of it by the box to distribute to friends, pestering book stores to order it, even volunteering to put up money to publicize it. His confidence in my skills and my future as a writer far exceeded my own.

On the surface, at least, our lives showed striking parallels. We had gone to the same boarding school and college. After college, we had both served in the military, were married as young officers, and, because of a war, endured forced separations from our wives. Within this biographical framework, however, the differences were at least as great as the similarities. He liked the southern boarding school we both attended, while as a Yankee—from New Jersey, no less—I was miserable there and despised what I regarded as its suffocating provincialism.

I assumed that Princeton would be better, and it was, although our careers there had little in common. He was a wrestler and a member of Tiger Inn, an eating club (the Princeton equivalent of fraternities) characterized by F. Scott Fitzgerald as "broad-shouldered and athletic." I was a non-jock, a would-be member of the campus literati, and belonged to Colonial Club, described by a magazine writer at the time as populated with "attenuated intellectuals"; I was at least attenuated.

While in college we both joined Army ROTC—my dad because he wanted to, I because he insisted on it. I loathed the scratchy uniforms, the inspections and close-order drill, the stupefying curriculum. The nadir of my cadet experience was something called the Fall Review, in which the school's Army, Navy, and Air Force ROTC units paraded in front of visiting brass. As part of the activities, our unit staged a field artillery exercise, and I had been assigned to the team charged with setting up and blank-firing a howitzer. A narrator explained the proceedings over a loudspeaker, then read the seconds off a stopwatch. The truck carrying the team careened onto the field with the howitzer in tow. It jolted to a stop and we leaped into action. Only I didn't leap: I fell, tripping on the tailgate and tumbling head over heels into the mud, losing my helmet and whatever dignity I had managed to carry into this charade of a military action.

The incident provoked howls of laughter from the cadets and other spectators and confirmed my growing suspicion that I wasn't cut out for the military.

"I hate ROTC," I told my father over Christmas vacation. "I know you want me to stay with it, but I can't stand it. I'd rather take my chances later trying to get into Navy OCS."

Against his better judgment, and to his everlasting credit, he let me quit.

In the spring of my senior year of college, I applied to Navy Officer Candidate School. By then, the country's deepening involvement in Vietnam had pushed up draft quotas, making Navy OCS fiercely competitive. By contrast, the Army and Marine Corps's officer schools were taking every warm body they could, but the notion of leading an infantry platoon in the swamps of Southeast Asia, in a war about which I felt a growing ambivalence, was singularly unappealing. If I couldn't avoid the draft—as most of my college friends managed to do, one way or another—I wanted at least to have some control over my destiny. But I was not sanguine about getting into the Navy because of my feeble eyesight, which was well below the OCS standard. I expected to flunk the eye exam for sure, and when, on a grim March day at the Philadelphia recruiting center, I took the physical, the letters on the screen were a hopeless blur. Yet to my surprise and relief, I was admitted into the program. My father had a friend from college, Robert Baldwin, who was serving as undersecretary of the Navy. Although I knew at the time that Dad had told him about my application to OCS, only later did I learn that I almost certainly owed my acceptance to his influence.

I have pondered the "what ifs" ever since. Among my other postgraduate options was teaching for a year at an American school in Beirut, Lebanon (at the time a peaceful country; it would be another decade before it would disintegrate into civil war). My acceptances from OCS and the school arrived concurrently. I wanted to have my cake and eat it, too. In order to take the school's offer, I considered asking the Navy for a one-year deferral from OCS but immediately thought better of it, fearing that such a request might send the wrong signal—maybe even cause the Navy to revoke my acceptance. So with some reluctance, I turned down the school's invitation to join its teaching staff. Another Princeton senior went in my place, taught for a year, was drafted and sent to Vietnam as an infantry platoon leader. Within a month of his arrival there, he was killed in action.

Prior to entering OCS in the fall of 1966, I spent a lonely, introspective summer living and working in Geneva, Switzerland. Although I didn't realize it at the time, this would be my final bout with the protracted disease called adolescence. At the end of the summer I spent an exhilarating sixteen days hitchhiking through northern Italy and up through France, flying home from Paris with ten centimes (about two cents) to my name. Less than a week later I was at OCS, at Newport, Rhode Island—head shaved and running around double-time, with student officers screaming at me and the others in my company. To my surprise, it wasn't nearly as bad as I had expected. In the military, I discovered, one's problems tend to be tangible, immediate, and usually solvable. Instead of fretting about what to make of my life, I worried about the quality of my spit-shine and whether my bunk was tight enough to bounce a quarter.

I liked the guys in my company and with most of them adopted a healthy irreverence toward the absurdities we found all around us. Our humor was good-spirited, even if more than a bit sophomoric, and it could take elaborate form. It was a truism that "OCS sucks," so much so that you could measure your degree of dissatisfaction—known as the "suck count"—on a device called a suckometer. Even in the best of moments you could always get a reading. "A suck count of zero is impossible," explained the author of this conceit—"like trying to achieve a perfect vacuum. Even after you leave the place, it stays with you, a kind of OCS half-life." The only way to avoid contamination, we decided, would be to send a "steamer body" through OCS in your place ("steamer" being navalese for substitute), then drive a stake through its heart and bury it deep underground in a lead casket.

In retrospect, most of us were having the time of our lives. I was happy being just one of the boys, except we were more than that. Like millions of American males in the twentieth century, I experienced military training as a rite of passage to manhood.

So I felt, anyway. My parents came to Newport in February 1967 to watch me graduate and receive my commission. My orders were to a destroyer escort patrolling off Vietnam; three months later, I boarded a military charter at Hamilton Air Force Base outside of San Francisco and flew via Alaska and Japan to Saigon, Vietnam. Although I didn't realize it at the time, twenty-three years before, what was then called Hamilton Field had been the point of embarkation for my dad and his crew.

■

On the afternoon of October 10, 1944, the *Liberty Belle* crewmen made a wide detour of the airfield captured earlier in the day by the Ustashi. The timing of the enemy's attack on the field suggested that they knew the Americans would be trying to rendezvous with a rescue plane. It was frustrating and depressing. The mood of the airmen wasn't helped by their wet clothes and lack of sleep, and the guide's assurance that they were just a day's walk from another airfield was, at best, mildly uplifting. A few miles farther on they stopped at a farmhouse and crawled into a hayloft for a nap. About two o'clock, the guide roused them. The woman of the house served up a plain but hearty meal of cottage cheese, butter, and hot bread before they hit the road again.

That evening they arrived at Duprava, a fair-sized town whose principal residence was a solid, two-story stucco house occupied by the local doctor and his family. The crew split into smaller groups, each assigned to a particular home for dinner. Merritt and Rudolph ate at the doctor's.

In Carl Rudolph's written narrative of their journey, he noted that the doctor spoke English and "had a very good meal prepared for us"—food never being far from Rudy's or anyone else's mind. He regarded the match-up with their host (the town's leading citizen) as a stroke of fortune, but he otherwise didn't elaborate on the visit. There was no mention of the doctor's family, which included a ten-year-old girl who stared at the Americans in wide-eyed wonder as her father pumped them for information about the war.

The doctor's name was Vjenceslav Chytil. He was a Czech by heritage, and along with English, Czech, and Serbo-Croatian he spoke German, French, and Greek. A Partisan sympathizer, he followed the war's progress on BBC broadcasts, noting changing battle lines and major engagements on a world atlas he kept by the radio. His daughter's name was Lydija, and like her father, she would grow up to be a physician.

■

Late in the afternoon of September 4, 1986, Dr. Lydija Chytil greeted us warmly in her apartment overlooking a shopping promenade in the city of Bjelovar. She was a pleasant woman in her early fifties, soft-spoken, and with an excellent command of English—a facility she shared with her tall, patrician husband and their twenty-three-year-old son, who was blond, self-possessed, and with flawless man-

ners. This was a family of doctors: Lydija Chytil ran a clinic
in Bjelovar, while her husband, a radiologist, worked at a
hospital in Zagreb. The son was a medical student in Zagreb
and had come for the day especially to meet us.

The apartment was comfortably bourgeois, and Dad
gladly accepted the scotch that was proffered—a choice of
Johnny Walker or Ballantine's, no less—and on the tray of
cordials there was not even a whiff of home-brewed *rakija*.
We were seated at the dining room table, which like the rest
of the furniture had been made in Vienna, Dr. Chytil told us,
and had once occupied her father's house in Duprava. We
were about fifteen miles from Duprava and planned to visit
there tomorrow to see the house and pay our respects at the
grave of the senior Chytil, who had died in 1958. Lydija
Chytil showed us a black-and-white photograph of the
house taken a few years after the war. By then it had been
rebuilt, following a direct hit by Stuka dive bombers (presumably flown by Ustashi, who must have been attacking
Duprava as a Partisan stronghold). Dominating one wall of
the room was a large seascape; she pointed out several small
holes in the canvas, the result of shrapnel.

Over the scotch, wine, and a tray of cookies, we talked
about the war and my father's and Rudy's visit to the Chytil
household.

"I remember two tall American fliers," Dr. Chytil said.
"My father was very glad to have someone to talk with
about the war. Our mother was a very good cook, and I
believe you enjoyed her dinner very much. After that you
had a bath, and one of you went to sleep."

"That must have been my navigator. Both he and my
bombardier could take a nap just like that," said Dad, snapping his fingers.

She brought out other items recalling her father—his

medical school diploma from the University of Zagreb and
the atlas he used to plot the Allies' progress. But what interested me most was a tiny circular object, no bigger than a
candy lifesaver. It took me a second to recognize it as a
pocket compass. I held it in the palm of my hand, its needle
quivering in its brass casing. It had come, I learned, from
Rudy's escape kit. He had presented it in gratitude to the
elder Chytil for his hospitality. The doctor and then his
daughter had kept it all these years, a memento of a brief
visit by two American airmen and the hope they inspired for
an Allied victory.

■

I had been looking forward to meeting Lydija Chytil since
the previous spring, when, following a silence of five
months, I heard again from Zerovc and Selhaus. In a letter,
Zerovc told me that the notice they had placed in the
Koprivnica paper had drawn a number of responses,
including one from Dr. Chytil. Most of the replies had come
from Koprivnica and vividly recalled the events surrounding
the *Liberty Belle*'s crash. I was astonished to read that
among those responding was a woman who had witnessed
"a plane on that day crashed down near her vineyard," a
former Partisan who "took down from the tree an airman,"
and two "natives from Kapela" who knew "the place where
the bomber downed."

A few weeks later, Zerovc wrote again:

> Since the last news to you, Edi Selhaus has got over thirty
> letters from the area of Koprivnica. The people write how
> they (some of them) contacted the airmen, and others
> remember them spending during first two days after

landing. So we decided to visit Koprivnica to look around
how much true is about those informations.

Enclosed in the letter were a dozen black-and-white photographs taken by Selhaus and Zerovc on their visit. One
showed a farmer with a discus-sized gear from one of the
Liberty Belle's engines; in another, a woman posed with a
serrated metal strip that looked like it might have been part
of the plane's control assembly. There were pictures of
Zerovc and Selhaus interviewing participants in the rescue,
visiting a farmhouse where the crew had hidden, and hiking
up a wooded hillside at the crash site.

In early July I heard directly from Selhaus, who by now
had received more than forty letters in response to his
notices and to a series of newspaper articles he had written
about the *Liberty Belle* based on his Koprivnica visit and on
materials I had sent him.

The rush of events forced a decision. During the months
of silence from Selhaus and Zerovc, I had been thinking
about making an exploratory trip to Yugoslavia by myself,
sometime in the next year or so. The idea would be to go
alone to see what I could find, with the possibility of
returning later with my dad and perhaps some other members of his crew. Now it seemed critical to take advantage of
the local interest generated by Selhaus and Zerovc. If I were
going to carry through on the project, I had better do so
quickly; that meant going to Yugoslavia sooner rather than
later, and not alone but with my father.

■

Dazed from jet lag, Dad and I stared dully from the window
of our Pan American jetliner as we approached the Zagreb

airport, early in the afternoon of September 2, 1986. We had left home twenty-seven hours before. The hazy country-side looked more or less as I imagined it, a quilt-work of farm fields and woods interspersed with tile-roofed houses. It had been forty-one years and ten months since my father had last laid eyes on this landscape.

Absorbed in the scene below, neither of us spoke. As the plane touched down and taxied to the terminal, I was wor-rying about details concerning our car rental, hotel reserva-tions, and the like. Dad, I learned later, was pondering what this airfield must have looked like in 1944, with Messer-schmitts taking off from it.

The next morning, Edi Selhaus and Janez Zerovc took the train from Ljubljana to rendezvous with us in Zagreb. They were to be our guides, and I knew from our correspon-dence that they had put together a loose itinerary that would start in Koprivnica and end in Casma, a former Partisan stronghold where the *Liberty Belle* crew had spent a fort-night before moving to the coast. For the last week I had been fretting about the trip, whose success or failure would rest on the groundwork laid by Selhaus and Zerovc. I was also concerned with Zerovc's language abilities, for he would be our interpreter. His native language was Slovene, and I had to trust that his speaking knowledge of both Eng-lish and Serbo-Croatian would be up to the task.

My concerns eased within minutes of the arrival of Zerovc and Selhaus at our room in the Hotel Inter-Continental. They appeared well organized, and Zerovc had at least a passing command of English. Moreover, they were a personable and engaging pair whose company, I sensed, we would enjoy in the days ahead. The more reserved of the two, Janez was about my age, of medium height, with thick dark hair and chiseled features. Married and the father of two boys, he worked as an engineer in a tool-and-die factory and was a pilot by avocation, with a consuming passion for flying and World War II aviation.

Like my father, Edi was in his mid-sixties and semi-retired—a hulking man with a ready smile and the disheveled appearance typical of nearly every newspaper photographer I have ever known. Edi had spent his life as a photojournalist and estimated that he had taken 2 million pictures in a career spanning nearly fifty years. His portfolio, he told us, included forty thousand photographs documenting the activities of Slovenian Partisans during the war—"I carried a camera in one hand and a gun in the other," he told us—and several hundred shots of Tito taken during the postwar years. An enthusiastic amateur photographer, the Yugoslav leader would occasionally grab Edi's camera and turn the lens on him.

In its details, Edi's life embodied a cultural and political flux that seemed remarkable, even by European standards. His mother and father (both photographers) were by nationality Italian and German, respectively. They raised their children in Ljubljana, and Edi grew up speaking fluent Italian, German, and Slovene. After the German invasion of Yugoslavia, Edi's brother wound up in the Wehrmacht and fought on the Eastern Front, where he was captured and spent the rest of the war as a prisoner of the Russians. Edi's mother fought for the Partisans, was captured, and finished the war as a prisoner of the Germans. After the war, Edi married an Italian and moved to Trieste, a border city then in contention between Italy and Yugoslavia. (After a period of civil unrest in which many Slovenes, Edi among them, were imprisoned, Trieste became part of Yugoslavia.) He and his wife had four children before they divorced and Edi returned to Ljubljana. Two of his children were still living, including a daughter who worked as a translator in Trieste. "She speaks many languages very well, but not the father language," he said, and when they talked to each other, it was not in Slovenian but in Italian.

Edi's command of spoken English was marginal, and most of our conversations were translated by Janez. The two had met ten years earlier as a result of Janez reading a magazine article by Edi recounting the rescue of a bomber pilot by a woman and her daughter. When readers began tipping him off about similar occurrences throughout Slovenia, Edi realized he was onto something. He began collecting rescue stories and wrote a series of articles, and ultimately a book, about them. As the resident authority and clearing house on the subject, he also took to orchestrating the occasional visit by former downed American fliers returning to Slovenia. In 1976, when two former Liberator crewmen, Gerard Armstrong of Cleveland and William Petty of Carthage, Tennessee, returned to the village of Dresnica, where they had hidden from the Germans, Selhaus arranged every detail of their visit, including a hike to the spot on Mt. Krn, in the Julian Alps, where their Liberator had crashed. Although nothing of the plane remained at the site, their guides showed them a barn whose door had been fashioned from the wing section, with the U.S. insignia—a white star in a circle of blue—still in place.

Janez had hiked in the Julian Alps since boyhood, and he knew the mountains well. With four like-minded friends, he organized the "Liberator Club" and began scouring the region for the remains of planes described in Edi's articles. "Many times we had to search a lot for the place where the bomber crashed," he said. They found their first plane in a remote valley at seventy-eight hundred feet on the Italian-Slovenian border. All that remained of it were bits of aluminum, an exhaust manifold, and some fifty-caliber shells. At another place they found parts of a fuselage, although at most of the dozen or so sites they investigated pickings were lean. Perhaps sixty bombers fell in Slovenia, but in every case, Janez said, local villagers descended on the wreckage "like ants," picking it clean. Pieces of wings and tails became roofs, gates, and doors or were hammered into cooking utensils and plates.

The four of us proceeded in our rental car to Koprivnica, a two-hour drive through rolling hills and endless corn ripening under a deep September sky. In 1944 the countryside had reminded my father of Piedmont Virginia, and so it seemed to me now. The main difference between then and now was the obvious prosperity. We drove on a paved road and passed tractors, and in the villages we noticed dogs. During the war, all the roads had been dirt, and even draft animals were in short supply, having been commandeered for food. I remembered one airman's description of a mother tilling a field with her daughter hitched to the plow—he fantasized about returning to Yugoslavia after the war as a distributor for Caterpillar Tractor. As for dogs, the *Liberty Belle* crewmen didn't recall seeing a single one during their stay in Yugoslavia; by then, most had wound up in the stew pot.

■

Our trip began in earnest on our arrival in Koprivnica, a nondescript provincial city dominated by a sprawling food-processing plant, the largest in Yugoslavia, with a giant wooden chicken outside it. Its population of twenty-three thousand, we were told, was more than three times what it had been during the war.

Edi's articles had made my dad a celebrity. The media—reporters, photographers, and a TV news crew from Zagreb—were waiting for him and followed us into our first meeting, which took place in the local veteran's hall. Seated with us at the conference table were several former members of a local Partisan unit that had assisted in the rescue of the *Liberty Belle* crew. One of them was Branko Vitanovic, a ruddy-faced man in his early seventies with a gap-toothed grin, gray moustache, and full gray hair swept straight back. "Every day we watched the bombers going overhead and were prepared, if a plane had troubles, to come to its rescue," he recalled.

Both Partisan and Ustashi units were in the area, with each faction patrolling its tenuously held territory. The *Liberty Belle*, we learned, crashed in Partisan territory, although just barely, and except for quick action by the Partisans all of its crew might have been captured by the Ustashi. Watching the crippled bomber's descent, Vitanovic said, "We first saw one man jump, then after some seconds the others followed." The Partisans rushed up the hill ahead of the Ustashi to collect the crewmen. "You were all very tall young boys," Vitanovic remembered. "'Tito—Partisans!' was all that we could say to you, as we didn't know any other English."

The memory evoked laughter from around the table. Vitanovic also recalled an exchange of pistols, the Partisans trading their thirty-caliber Berettas (captured from Italian troops) for the American's heftier forty-five-caliber Colts.

"I remember that now," Dad said. "We got these very small pistols in exchange for our very big pistols."

"There were many Allied soldiers crossing our area," Vitanovic continued. "Some of them were escaping prisoners of war, others were airmen. Many came from Slovenia. There were English, Americans, French, and Russians. Some of them were wounded, and I remember one American who died and was buried in Poganac. We helped them all with clothes, food, and medicine. Our main job was to escort them safely to the next area."

"You speak of how young my crew was," Dad said, "but they weren't nearly as young as the twelve-year-old Partisan boys I saw who bragged about killing Germans. That really surprised us, along with the number of women soldiers. Some of them were very pretty, but we always understood that there was no hanky-panky between them and the men."

"By hanky-panky he means sex," I said.

Vitanovic smiled. "We had a rule that anyone having sex must be shot. Everyone was very happy just to stay alive."

More laughter. I was tempted to mention (but refrained from doing so, even though it was common knowledge) that Tito himself, who kept a mistress-cum-secretary throughout the war, was perhaps the most conspicuous violator of the Partisan sex ban.

Vitanovic's description of a break in the bailout sequence—"We first saw one man jump, *then after some seconds* the others . . ." [emphasis added]—jibed with the accounts of the *Liberty Belle* crewmen, and for the first time I realized how critical the timing had been. Carver, the tail gunner, had jumped first, while the plane was still over Ustashi territory. The others would have followed immediately and like Carver probably would have been captured, except for the delay caused by Wheeler's hesitation before he was booted from the plane. This pause in the sequence could not have been more than a few seconds, since, according to the Missing Air Crew Report, as they descended in their parachutes, Carver had been close enough to the next man in line to exchange a wave. I calculated that, during the gap between Carver's exit and the rest of the crew's, the plane may have traveled fifteen hundred feet or less—enough, barely, to get it over Partisan territory.

The session ended with the obligatory round of *rakija* and toasts. "I am very grateful for the assistance you gave us in 1944," Dad said. "Without it, we might not be here today."

■

We assembled outside the veteran's hall for photographs, then drove into the countryside to talk with others who helped in the rescue and escape. The people we met on this and the following two days included Milan Suka. Stout, tanned, and with thick gray hair and glasses, Suka had been nineteen years old in 1944 and a member of a Partisan unit in Vrhovac. We gathered in the small family room of his farmhouse for *rakija,* coffee, sliced ham, tomatoes, cottage cheese, and strudel. Four generations of Suka women—his aged, black-shawled mother-in-law and his wife, daughter, and granddaughter—crowded into the doorway to listen to the animated talk, but they never entered the conversation themselves.

Like many of those serving in the Partisan forces in this area, Suka was a member of the region's ethnic Serbian minority, despised by the native Croats. "When the Ustashi took over, they killed many of our people and destroyed our churches," he said. "The Communist Party was the main organizer here and had no trouble recruiting young men whose homes had been burned and families killed."

On the afternoon the *Liberty Belle* went down, he recalled, "We were in the village, and when we saw the plane coming low over the hills we went running immediately in its direction. The Partisan and Ustashi units were perhaps five minutes apart, and it was a question of which of them would get there first. We found nine of your crew, but we didn't have time to find the tenth. I am pleased to know that all of you survived the war. After you left this area, we talked many times about your escape and always wondered what happened to you."

■

Andrija Celescek was a member of the unit that escorted the *Liberty Belle* crew south from Topolovac through St. Ivan Zabno and Duprava and on to the regional Partisan headquarters at Casma. A small, erect man in a suit and tieless white shirt buttoned at the collar, he met us in the offices of *Glas Podravina*, the local newspaper, on the second morning of our stay in Koprivnica. Sitting across a coffee table from us in the spartan office of the managing editor, Celescek was polite and reserved, with a twinkle in his eye. He and my dad got on instantly, each bragging to the other of their families. He went on at length about his two daughters—one an engineer, the other a travel agent—and his grandsons, ages ten months and two years.

In October 1944 he was a twenty-two-year-old corporal who had been with the Partisans about a year. When I asked one of my standard questions—Why did you join the Partisans?—he smiled. "That is a funny story."

He had started the war as a Ustashi conscript, he said, and volunteered for the Devil Brigade, a Wehrmacht unit composed of Croatian nationals. Trained as a mechanic, he was stationed first in Austria and then in Bavaria before being reassigned to Croatia.

"In Germany and Austria," he said, "we wore German uniforms with a Croatian arm patch. After we came home, we wanted to wear our own uniforms, but the Germans wouldn't allow it. I no longer wanted anything to do with the Germans and began thinking about joining the Partisans."

When Celescek requested a five-day leave to return to his home in Koprivnica, his commanding officer became suspicious and sent three German soldiers to accompany him. Two of them eventually returned to the unit, but the third stayed with Celescek, with instructions to keep an eye on him. Celescek plied his guard with *rakija* until he passed out, then stole his pistol, hopped on a bicycle, and peddled out of town and to the nearest Partisan unit to enlist. When the German came to with a pounding hangover, he found himself a prisoner of Celescek and his new Partisan comrades.

■

Milka Drazina, who on the day of the crash was making wine in a hillside vineyard with other women, some children, and older men, saw the plane stagger overhead and watched, amazed, as one of the airmen floated down in their midst. The airman was Wheeler, and she gave him wine and fruit while tending to his injured hand.

Drazina was twenty-five years old at the time and married to a Partisan stationed in another part of the country. Now widowed, she had a sweet smile and reddish brown hair, whose lack of gray made her appear younger than she must have been. When we visited her in her cottage outside Koprivnica, she showed us a family photo album with a picture of her husband in his Partisan uniform, with a German assault rifle slung from his neck. The room was filled with mementos of him—shotguns in the corner, a stuffed pheasant and hawk, and a glass display case full of war medals.

"He was a good soldier and a good farmer," she said. "I am alone now, but this is the happiest day for me. I have been waiting forty years to see one of these Americans again."

Much later, Edi sent to me a fuller account of her recollections, based on what she had said on the day of our visit and on an earlier interview he had had with her. As I read Edi's account, it became obvious that I had missed something in the translation; or perhaps Edi was incurably romantic and inferred a lot more from her story. Anyway, according to Edi, she recalled October 7, 1944, as a beautiful autumn day in the midst of the grape harvest. The warm weather and the task at hand put everyone in a pleasant mood in spite of the war, and in the morning, the sight of the American bombers on their way north cheered them even more. "They represented hope to us, and made the end of the war seem very near," she told Edi.

In the afternoon, they watched the formations returning

and noticed one plane flying much lower and far behind the rest. They heard the bomber crash in the forest and watched the parachutes bloom behind it. Two of the airmen landed in the vineyard where Milka was working. She remembered one with an injured hand (Wheeler) and another who landed "right in front of Kosuta's wine cellar, which he entered after he got rid of his parachute. There was a large keg of fermenting juice, and I remember him drinking it from a pail."

The airman in the wine cellar was "tall and handsome," she told Edi. Over the years she had never forgotten him. She was even in love with him, or at least with his image and its association with her youth. She spoke often of the airman with her mother, who on her death bed told Milka, "Have faith, he will come again."

Seeing my father on the day of our visit, she said to Edi: "That's him—he's still as handsome as I remembered. I know it was he who landed in our vineyard."

I took this bit of melodrama on faith. Milka Drazina seemed a sincere woman, and even if my dad and I had understood all of her story at the time we met her, I'm sure we would not have had the heart to disabuse her of it. Unfortunately, the part about the handsome airman failed to jibe with my father's account of his first moments on the ground. Nor did it fit well with the stories of Martin and Corbo, the other crewmen who told me of landing on or near a vineyard.

So who was this striking airman whose image she had cherished all these years? I will probably never know. Perhaps it was either Cunningham or Dupree, the two crewmen I had failed to locate. But Rudolph recalled Cunningham landing in a stream, not a vineyard. By default, that left

Dupree, the one member of the crew for whom the record remains blank.

■

Another Partisan, Zarko Gudek, was leading a six-man intelligence unit on the day the *Liberty Belle* went down. The photographs Edi had sent to me before our trip included a wartime portrait of Gudek; in his Partisan uniform, draped with a Schmeisser assault rifle taken off a dead SS trooper, he stared with chilling intensity at the camera, a central-casting version of a guerrilla fighter.

The handsome young soldier in the photograph was still recognizable in the vigorous older man who greeted us with a hearty grin in the courtyard of his arbor-bedecked farmhouse. He wore a striped shirt over his prosperous girth, and he fairly enveloped us in his double handshake. I noticed that one of his index fingers was missing and that he walked with a limp—the result, I learned, not of some wartime action but of a farming accident.

Gudek and my dad hit it off immediately. At six-foot-two, the ex-pilot stood several inches taller than his rescuer; Dad looked hail and fit and robustly patrician with his pewter temples, snappy peaked cap, khaki raincoat, and creased twill pants, so similar to the Air Corps "pinks" I remembered from his old uniform.

Gudek recalled in detail the events of October 7, 1944, which resulted not only in my father's rescue but in the advancement of his own career. He and his men had been in the area for several days assessing Ustashi strength. Patrolling on a wooded hillside northeast of Vrhovac, they watched the waves of bombers returning from Austria and noticed—well behind the others and at a much lower altitude—the crippled Liberator. Anticipating that the plane would probably crash near the border between Ustashi and Partisan territories, they prepared for a rescue. Moments later, a line of parachutes bloomed behind the plane as it banked and exploded on the ridge above.

"I turned to my comrade, Feliks Kucan, who I knew was the fastest, and ordered him to run to our headquarters to get some extra help," Gudek told us. Kucan hadn't gone far before meeting some other Partisans ascending the hill.

From their position on the hill, Gudek's men fought off a Ustashi patrol, spraying the woods below them with the submachine gun fire heard by descending *Liberty Belle* crewmen.

The two Partisan units in the area (Gudek's and Branko Vitanovic's) rounded up the crewmen and hurried them through the woods to Vrhovac. Like Vitanovic, Gudek had watched Carver land at some distance from the others, too far for his men to reach him before the Ustashi. "We tried to get to him but were too late," Gudek said, a frown crossing his weathered face. "I was very angry about this at the time, and I am still very angry about it today."

Recognizing his initiative, the Partisan command presented Gudek with a medal and invited him to join the Communist Party. He showed us his membership credentials, a little red booklet engraved with a picture of Tito. "This was the greatest honor for me," he said.

We went inside for coffee and the inevitable *rakija* toasts. My dad, who favors Irish coffee, mixed the two: "This is what you call Yugoslav coffee," he said. Gudek's daughter, a physician who worked in Koprivnica, was visiting for the occasion and served us, but like the women in Suka's home, she stayed out of the conversation. With a picture of Tito looking down at us from the wall (an official portrait of the Yugoslav leader hung in every house we entered), Dad and Gudek stood up to exchange mementos—the pilot presenting his rescuer with a pewter tie clasp in the shape of a B-24, and the old Partisan reciprocating with a gold lapel pin, a facsimile of Tito's signature.

"*Palo lepa!*—Good friend!" exalted Gudek, grabbing my father in a bear hug. Dad's natural reserve gave way as he returned the embrace with a grin. It was a moment that in my wildest imaginings I never thought to see—my conservative Republican father in the arms of a card-carrying Communist. I was reminded of one of the staples in his repertoire of Yugoslavia stories. Whenever the *Liberty Belle* crewmen entered a Partisan village, the people would shout to the visiting Americans, "Roosevelt! Roosevelt!" Invariably during that election-year fall of 1944, my father would respond with the name of the Republican candidate, shouting back, "Dewey! Dewey!" to the uncomprehending Yugoslavs.

Whatever he thought of their political system, Dad admired the Yugoslav people, who following the war were the only East European Communists to break with Moscow. "You are the only country I know that told both Hitler and Stalin to go to hell," he said. "What other country can say that?"

Chapter 5
DUPRAVA TO MIKLOUS

After saying goodbye to Dr. Chytil and his family, Merritt and Rudolph rejoined the rest of the *Liberty Belle* crew at the house of a local official. They had hoped to rest for the night in Duprava, but the Partisans had other plans for them. Reluctantly they climbed aboard the wagons and moved out in the drizzly night toward Casma, a Partisan town about ten miles to the south. The convoy arrived there at about three in the morning, and to the airmen's astonishment they found steak dinners awaiting them, courtesy of the local Partisan garrison. After filling their bellies they collapsed on straw spread on the floor of the Partisan barracks and slept until ten the next morning.

When they awoke, the skies were clearing. It was the first they had seen of the sun for three days, and their mood was upbeat as they hit the road again. Their destination was the village of Miklous, five miles away, where the Partisans maintained another airfield. Maybe at this very moment a plane was flying in to rescue them! But their spirits plunged at the sight of the rain-soaked runway, and they resigned themselves to being in Yugoslavia at least for a few more days. At Casma, a British secret-service officer had taken their names and had promised to send a message to Bari about their whereabouts; at least, they figured, the Fifteenth Air Force would know they were safe and would so inform their next-of-kin.

At Miklous, the Partisans put them up among three cottages. The straw mattresses in the cottage shared by Merritt, Rudolph, and Maes looked inviting but turned out to be infested with lice, a fact they did not discover until they awoke scratching in the middle of the night. Over the next two weeks they settled into the tedium of waiting for the rains to cease and the airfield to dry sufficiently for a plane to land and take off. They were all crawling with lice and suffering from chronic diarrhea and losing weight. They smelled like pigs. The sour weather reflected their mood, for the rains continued on and off, dimming their hope of evacuation any time soon. Still, life was not entirely unpleasant, for at least no one was shooting at them. As Rudolph later recalled, "Spare time, which was most of the time, was spent playing hearts, drinking vena, shooting chickens, smoking foul cigarettes, and going to the john." They played touch football with a sock stuffed with straw and helped the locals harvest apples and potatoes. Cooking for them was a middle-aged woman named Marie. Her specialty was apple strudel, made with dark flour and precious sugar haggled from the Brits in Casma. For the rest of his life, Nick Corbo couldn't eat strudel without thinking of her. They came to look on Marie as a surrogate mother, even if her sanitary standards were not exactly up to Mom's. As Rudolph noted, "the horde of flies on the food and walls didn't bother her a bit."

Although Miklous and its surrounding countryside were peaceful, the war was never far off. One night they listened to distant rumbling and watched a glow on the horizon as Allied bombers pounded Zagreb. Almost daily, German planes—Dornier 217s and Junker Trimotors ferrying troops and supplies—lumbered overhead. Even before he saw the planes, Merritt always recognized them from their sing-song caterwaul; he couldn't understand why the Luftwaffe pilots never bothered to synchronize their propellers.

On the night of October 20 they knocked down a gallon of wine. While sleeping it off they were startled awake by shouting and the rat-tat-tat of automatic weapons.

Several of them would later remember the incident as one of the few times in Yugoslavia when they felt in real danger. Martin dove under a bed, convinced a Panzer division had hit the village. Maes whipped out the Beretta he had traded for his service automatic and aimed at the door, expecting any second for someone to fling it open and toss in a grenade. After a few moments, it dawned on him that the yelling lacked the urgency of battle and that the tracers he saw cutting across the night sky were arcing at steep angles, more like fireworks. All the commotion, it turned out, was just the Partisans celebrating the capture of Belgrade, the Yugoslav capital.

■

The fall of Belgrade was Tito's greatest victory of the war, and it spelled the end of German domination of the Balkans, a region controlled by the Nazis since their invasion of Yugoslavia and Greece in the spring of 1941.

In Greece, the political and military situation for the last three and a half years had been at least as complicated as that in Yugoslavia. Like the Yugoslavs, the Greeks had been waging a civil war within an occupied country, with Communist and centrist guerrillas fighting each other as well as the Germans. In the spring of 1944, George Papandreou, prime minister of the Greek government-in-exile, succeeded in uniting, however tenuously, his country's rival factions in order to drive the Germans from their soil.

By this point in the war the Yugoslavian Partisans had four hundred thousand men and women under arms and were continuing to grow rapidly. They controlled most of the mountainous central region of Bosnia, as well as sizable portions of Croatia and Slovenia, and enjoyed the support of the British and Americans, who were air-dropping three thousand tons of supplies to them every month. Abandoned by the Allies, the rival Chetniks were confined to parts of Serbia and found themselves increasingly thrust into an uneasy collaboration with the Nazis. Despite the fickleness of Allied support, American airmen who fell into Chetnik hands could still count on friendly treatment. Mihailovic's forces rescued six hundred fliers during the war, and as late as August 1944 Chetnik units were protecting two hundred and fifty bomber crewmen shot down on raids on the Romanian oil fields at Ploesti. In one especially daring mission, the Fifteenth Air Force landed a dozen C-47 transports at a secret airfield near Belgrade and evacuated all of the fliers.

In September, the Partisans thrust east from their Bosnian stronghold into Serbia. This major offensive, code-named Operation Ratweek by the British, was meant to harass German troops who, to avoid being cut off by the Red Army rolling across Romania, had begun a general withdrawal from Greece. The Partisans saw Ratweek as an opportunity to destroy the weakened Chetnik army. Responding to Tito's promise of amnesty, many Chetniks abandoned Mihailovic and joined the Partisans, further swelling the Communist ranks. By early October, Russian units had crossed the Danube and with the Partisans were pressing on the capital. By the end of the month, the red star flew over Belgrade.

■

The momentum of the war was now with the Partisans, and to press their advantage they enlisted anyone willing to fight for their cause: refugees and prisoners of war escaping from territories liberated by the advancing Russians, captured Ustashi and Chetniks and foreign nationals in the Wehrmacht's occupation forces, even the occasional turncoat German or Austrian.

The pool of potential recruits included the hundreds of downed American airmen wandering the countryside. "One afternoon a Partisan hiked us off to a town about five miles away called Berek," Rudolph remembered. "One by one we were interrogated by a Yugoslavian officer and interpreter. They asked a lot of foolish questions; one in particular I remember was: 'Do you want to stay and fight with the Partisan army?'"

Nick Corbo, for one, listened politely and replied that they were all "highly trained technicians" who would serve the Yugoslavs better by returning to flying duty. Following an apple fight, they walked back to Miklous, wondering what was cooking for dinner.

The Partisans operated an officer training school in Miklous. It was located in the only building in town connected to a power plant some miles away, in territory controlled by the Ustashi, who knew that the Partisans were tapping electricity for the school. The Ustashi could have easily cut the line but chose not to because they also knew that the Partisans would almost certainly blow up the power plant in reprisal. A Mexican standoff, Balkan-style.

One night, Rudolph recalled, the *Liberty Belle* crewmen attended a dinner for the school's graduating class "and danced with a few of the local girls to the tune of a squeeze box. All I can say was that they were big gals."

Keith Martin remembered another occasion in Miklous when the Partisans put on a show for them. "It was in a barn, with a kind of stage set up. We went there at night even though it was hazardous to walk around after dark. Someone was always challenging you with '*Stoy!*'— 'Halt!'—and sticking a machine gun in your nose. The Partisans performed some folk dances, and to reciprocate, six or seven of us got up there and sang this song. Something like "There was an old farmer who had an old sow . . . ,' with all kinds of barnyard sounds—mooing and snorting—thrown in. The Partisans laughed and laughed."

■

September 5, 1986: on the afternoon of our third full day in Yugoslavia, we drove south from Koprivnica, stopping first at Duprava to see the house of the late Dr. Chytil, which looked unchanged from the forty-year-old photographs his daughter had showed us during our visit with her the day before. From Duprava we proceeded on to Casma, a prosperous-looking town dominated by the twin towers of its Catholic church. Edi and Janez had arranged a visit with a former Partisan named Dragutin Vukovic, a cheerful, energetic man in his early sixties, whose brigade was responsible for the *Liberty Belle* crewmen during their stay in the Casma-Miklous area.

In the bright, spacious kitchen we sat down to a midday dinner of ham, onions, cottage cheese, and—shades of the celebrated Marie—apple strudel. The ham came from pigs raised on Vukovic's farm, he noted proudly. "The Casma region has always been a very rich part of our country," he said. "Even during the worst part of the war, people could always count on something to eat here."

Joining us at the table were his son and daughter-in-law. They had come for the occasion from Zagreb, where the son worked in the meat-packing industry. It was a weekday, but he had taken time off from his job to be here. The elder Vukovic laid before us his service medals and began to reminisce about the war. "Our brigade blew up more trains than any other in the Partisan army," he said. "During this period, there were many American airmen passing through here. Seeing you made us feel very good—your presence reminded us that we were all in the same fight against Hitler."

Although not specifically recalling the *Liberty Belle* crew, he did remember several P-51 pilots from the 332nd Fighter Group, the all-Negro outfit that flew escort on my dad's Vienna mission. Like most Yugoslavians in 1944, Vukovic had never encountered a black person and was astonished at the sight.

The black pilots joined the *Liberty Belle* crewmen either in Miklous or Garesnica, a town where they spent a week after leaving Miklous. I recalled from childhood my father talking about them. Other airmen I interviewed also remembered the black pilots, although no one seemed to have known them more than casually, the racial barriers of that era precluding fraternization. There were three pilots, all members of the 332nd's 99th Fighter Squadron: Ruall W. Bell, of Portland, Oregon; Robert C. "Clair" Chandler, of Allegan, Michigan; and Shelby F. Westbrook, of Toledo, Ohio. Bell was shot down ten miles northeast of Zagreb on October 14, a week to the day after the *Liberty Belle* went down. Bad weather forced Chandler and Westbrook to land at a Partisan airfield on October 23, and once they were on the ground the muddy runway prevented them from taking off.

Most of what I knew about Chandler and Westbrook was based on phone conversations I had with both men in 1995, nine years after our trip to Yugoslavia. I was able to find them thanks to the assistance of George Watson, of Lakewood, New Jersey, and William A. Campbell, of Seaside, California. Both were members of the Tuskegee Airmen, a veterans organization representing the black airmen who had trained at the Tuskegee Institute, the college in Alabama founded by Booker T. Washington. Chandler, who was living in his boyhood home of Allegan when I spoke to him, spent thirty days on the ground in Yugoslavia. After rejoining their unit, he, Westbrook, and Bell returned to flight duty and finished out the war in Italy.

My dad put his recollections of the 332nd pilots in a letter he wrote to me shortly after my initial interview with him and Carl Rudolph. He remembered them as "first-class people" who were "subjects of many stares and comments by amazed Yugoslavs" who had never seen a black person before. (While this was generally true, Westbrook said the first Yugoslavian he met had lived in the United States so was quite familiar with African-Americans.) Dad had long ago forgotten their names but recalled one of them as being from Chicago—this might have been Chandler, since Allegan is about seventy miles from there. He remembered the other pilot being from Atlanta, but as it turned out, Dad was apparently confusing either Westbrook or Bell with another black airman he encountered after returning stateside, in December 1944. After disembarking from their troop ship in New York City, both Dad and the airman in question were shipped to Camp Shanks, New York, and then to Fort McPherson, Georgia, where they were granted thirty-day leaves.

Fort McPherson, of course, was deep in the segregated South. "It was sickening," wrote Dad, "to see the degrading treatment" the black pilot received from "the redneck sergeant who met our train." The story I remembered from childhood had them getting off the train and being directed by a southern sergeant to buses that would take them to a processing center. When the black pilot stepped off the train, the sergeant motioned him aside.

"Hold it, lieutenant. We've got another bus for you over here!"

No one—not the black officer or my father or anyone else—questioned either the sergeant's authority or a system declaring that black servicemen, including decorated combat veterans, weren't fit to ride in the same bus with whites. From today's moral perspective it is easy to condemn this incident, but it is difficult to imagine it resolving itself in any other way; if I had been in my father's shoes, I would have behaved no differently. Yet I have always fantasized a Hollywood ending to the story, with Dad telling off the redneck sergeant and insisting that the black pilot accompany him on the white servicemen's bus.

■

In addition to the black P-51 pilots, two other groups of airmen joined the *Liberty Belle* crew during its stay in Miklous.

Lieutenant Mike Spellacy's crew was flying its second mission on an inauspicious Friday, October 13. The target was Vienna, and they were hit the second after releasing their bombs, a burst of flak opening up the back of the plane like a sardine can and knocking out the oxygen and hydraulic systems, the radio, and two of the four engines. With the bomber streaming fuel, they dropped out of the formation and began the long descent toward Yugoslavia.

Checking the intercom, Spellacy was relieved to find that no one was injured. The ball-turret gunner panicked when he glanced down and saw that his flight suit was soaked in "blood," which turned out to be hydraulic fluid. When they got ready to bail out, the seventeen-year-old tail gunner glanced out the escape hatch, thought better of it, and crawled back into his turret. The two waist gunners yanked him back and pushed him out the hatch.

Spellacy rode the plane alone for several minutes before bailing out. He came down about ten miles from the rest of the crew, near the village of Trnovitica. His chute took two strong pulls on the ripcord to open. Like a weight at the end of a pendulum, he swung wildly on the descent. He heard dogs barking as the ground loomed closer. Landing in trees next to a road, he was startled by the roar of aircraft engines and looked up to see the friendly silhouettes of two P-51 Mustangs. The sleek fighters buzzed him at treetop level, then climbed steeply and made a beeline back to Italy. Until this instant, he had been unaware that these guardian angels had been riding shotgun all the way from Vienna.

He released himself from the parachute harness, fell to

the ground, and commenced running through the woods, away from the voices he heard on the road, until he came out on a path where an older man—he looked in his fifties—was standing. Like a specter, the man said nothing, but smiled and motioned for him to follow. Soon they came upon a second man, who appeared about the same age as the first. He wore a black, threadbare suit with gold buttons up the front. Spellacy recognized the outfit as the uniform of a train conductor, and he was astonished when the man spoke to him in fluent English.

"Where am I?" Spellacy asked.

"Congratulations—you've landed in Croatia!"

He explained that, for fifteen years, he had lived in Milwaukee, where he had worked for a railroad line. He had returned to Yugoslavia for a visit and became trapped there by the German invasion.

The former conductor was an ethnic Serb and as such was treated with contempt by the local Croats. When Spellacy innocently remarked on the beauty of the countryside, the Serb spat out: "I'd sooner be dead in America than alive over here!"

About a dozen Partisans and villagers had collected by now, and as a group they set off along the wooded path. They stopped at a farm house. By now Spellacy had a raging thirst, and when proffered a glass of clear liquid, he gulped it down in a few gulps. If he had been a cartoon character, smoke might have poured from his ears. The glass was filled with *rakija*.

Soon they arrived at Trnovitica, a village of ten thatched-roof cottages surrounding a communal well. The mayor had the largest house and barn as well as an ancient threshing machine that he showed off to his American guest. Spellacy's plane had crashed on a nearby hillside, and they hiked over to inspect its remains. Unlike the *Liberty Belle*, the bomber had not exploded on impact, although the engines and nose section had sheared off and were lying in a ravine.

The villagers sifted through the wreckage, salvaging anything they could carry away. Oxygen bottles, machine guns, ammunition belts, and other booty were soon heaped in front of the mayor's house. The Partisan captain, an officious sort detested by the Serbian conductor, spotted a distress pistol and grabbed it from the refuse pile. The scene that ensued might have sprung from the brain of Mack Sennett.

"He wants to know if he can shoot it," the Serb said.

"He can do whatever he wants—I don't care," replied Spellacy.

With a show of importance, the Partisan captain ordered everyone to stand back. He fired into the air. The cartridge shot up several hundred feet and at the top of its trajectory popped open, emitting a small parachute with a lighted flare swinging from the bottom.

Everyone cheered, and only Spellacy seemed to notice that the flare was descending toward one of the thatched roofs.

"It's going to land on the roof and start a fire!" he told the Serb.

"Who cares?" his friend replied. "It serves the big loudmouth right!"

Spellacy watched the flare float down onto the thatch. The roof leapt into flame and the fire brigade went into action. The villagers hauled out a pump wagon from a shed next to the mayor's house, threw the hose down the well, and pumped like mad. An anemic stream poured onto the cottage while the woman of the house ran out the back door, shooing a cow ahead of her.

Meanwhile, Spellacy had noticed a fire extinguisher in the heap of equipment salvaged from the plane. He pointed it out to the Serb, who told the Partisan captain. Snatching the extinguisher from the pile, the captain waved everyone out of the way and ran up to the flaming cottage. But all his vigorous pumping produced barely a trickle.

While flame consumed the cottage, Spellacy worried that, because he had given permission to shoot the distress pistol, he would be blamed for the catastrophe.

"Don't worry," the Serb assured him. "It's the bigshot captain's fault, not yours."

That night, as the village's guest of honor, Spellacy slept in the mayor's bed . . . with the mayor as his bedmate. The next morning, the Serb appeared at the window and handed him a hard-boiled egg.

"Don't share it with anyone," he said. "It's just for you!"

■

Mike Spellacy related this story in a letter he wrote to me from his home in San Diego, where he had retired several years before from the presidency of a trucking company in Minneapolis. I had learned of his whereabouts from his former flight engineer and top-turret gunner, Martin Kornbluh, a name I had come across in the packet of documents sent to me by the Air Force Archives. The materials included an escape statement by Kornbluh which one of the Air Force researchers had found serendipitously while looking for information related to my father. In 1944, when the debriefing officer at the Fifteenth Air Force's headquarters in

Bari had taken Kornbluh's statement, he had added to it notations from a diary kept by the gunner while in Yugoslavia. One of the entries noted that in Miklous they had

Here met Merritt's crew with Corbo as engineer with only one [man] missing. Marie cooks a good strudel! Rain spoils runway. Dysentery hits me & it's awful.

The statement listed Kornbluh's home in 1944 as Passaic, New Jersey, a town in the New York metropolitan area just five miles from Verona, where my parents lived. On the remote chance that he might still be living there, I checked the telephone directory for Passaic County. Although there was no listing for a Martin Kornbluh in the town of Passaic, I did find one for that name in the neighboring community of Clifton. When I called that evening, Mrs. Kornbluh answered. Her husband was still at work, she said, but would be back soon. When I told her my purpose, she confirmed that I had the right person.

"Marty will be very interested in this!"

Martin Kornbluh returned my call shortly after. He turned out to be the manager of a catering business on Bloomfield Avenue in Verona; for the last twenty years he had worked less than a mile from my parents' home.

Six weeks later, I drove up to Verona to meet Kornbluh at his business, stopping first at my parents' house to pick up Dad.

The catering business that Marty worked for was in an imposing white building with spacious ballrooms hung with floor-to-ceiling mirrors and crystal chandeliers. We found him in a small office in the back, a short, meticulous man with silvery hair, dressed in a blue blazer and gray slacks. He greeted us casually, as though this sort of thing occurred every day. Although he did not say so specifically, I sensed that he did not remember my father. He did recall Corbo, who as flight engineer had been his counterpart aboard the *Liberty Belle.*

We sat at a table in one of the empty reception areas and reminisced. Marty had brought with him a briefcase full of war-related materials, including vintage photographs, clippings, and a souvenir book of the Fifteenth Air Force in Italy. Just the night before, he said, he had called Mike Spellacy, in San Diego, to tell him about our visit. Although they had corresponded over the years, it was the first time since the war that he and his former pilot had actually spoken. Spellacy had kept up with most of the crew, all but two of whom were still living. One of the deceased, the ball-turret gunner, had died within the last few months.

Marty had grown up in Passaic, the son of a restaurateur, and had briefly studied architecture at a technical college in Newark, New Jersey, before entering the service in 1943 as a flight cadet in Santa Ana, California.

"The instructor swore I'd kill myself if I ever tried to solo," he said. "I was all stiff and would hang on to the controls of the Stearman trainer—the easiest plane in the world to fly—like I was driving a Model A back home. After I washed out of pilot training, they sent me to navigator's school. I was good enough at navigating from the ground, but once I got in the air and poked my head into the bubble, I could never get my bearings. Every star looked alike, and the more I tried to analyze my position, the sicker I got. At that point, it seemed like everyone washing out of navigator's school was going straight into the infantry. I was one of the lucky ones who got into flight engineer's school."

He wound up with a B-24 crew in Sacramento and was

ready to ship with it to the Eighth Air Force, in England, when he came down with a case of hemmorhoids. "That kept me stateside for another few weeks, until I joined Mike's crew and shipped to Italy. Meanwhile, my original crew had arrived overseas. Two weeks later they were blown up over Germany, with no survivors."

On his ill-fated mission of Friday the thirteenth, Marty was at his flight engineer's station, just aft of the pilot and copilot, when Spellacy told the crew to prepare to bail out. "I didn't wear a parachute during the flight but kept a chest pack handy," he said. "When Mike gave the word, I grabbed for the chest pack but kicked it by mistake, and it sprang open. Fortunately, I always kept several extra parachutes on the flight deck. I snapped on a seat pack—it was way too big for me, but I didn't dare try to adjust it. When I jumped, I was lucky it didn't tear my balls off. I'm left-handed and had trouble with the ripcord, and the brass handle hit me in the mouth. I remember tasting blood, although I wasn't badly hurt."

His descent, like Spellacy's, was greeted by a chorus of barking dogs. He landed in a vineyard, and like several of the *Liberty Belle* crewmen, he just missed being impaled on a sharpened grape stake. "Then I saw people with rifles and pitchforks running toward me. I raised my hands—'Americanski!'"

The Yugoslavs couldn't resist pulling the *rakija* joke; Kornbluh downed a glass of the firewater and passed out. "The next thing I remembered was waking up on the floor of a cottage to the sound of Partisans singing."

■

My father did not recall Mile Spellacy, Marty Kornbluh, or other members of their crew. Nor did Carl Rudolph mention them in his narrative, "The Walk Back," even though the two crews traveled along the same route at approximately the same time and shared many of the same experiences in Miklous and at other stops. There were probably several reasons for this—the crews were billeted in different places, and the insularity typical of military units tended to isolate one group from another.

Dad did remember the other crew that joined them in Miklous, however, perhaps because of the harrowing nature of their bailout. He recalled that the crew's pilot was named Lane—"a tall, good-looking Irishman," whose plane had run out of fuel on the flight home. Lane and his crew bailed out at a high altitude, making them irresistible targets for German gunners on the ground. When the crew assembled, three were missing. Based on the testimony of Partisans, it was assumed that they had been shot and killed, either in their parachutes while descending or as soon as they had touched down.

When I began my research, I knew that other crews had joined the men of the *Liberty Belle*. From the National Archives I obtained all the Missing Air Crew Reports that were available for planes that went down in Yugoslavia during October and November 1944. One of them listed as pilot a Homer W. Lane of New York City. According to the report, Lane had flown his last mission on Friday, October 13; this was the same day as Spellacy's mission, although his target—oil refineries at Bleckhammer, Germany—was different. The report included testimony from individual crewmen, made after their return to Italy, that focused on the fate of the missing copilot, engineer, and ball-turret gunner. As I read through the materials, it became clear that the Partisans were wrong about the three men being killed; in fact, all had been captured and interned as prisoners of war.

The last document in the report was a typewritten letter dated March 2, 1946 (nine months after the war ended) and addressed to a lieutenant colonel in the Personal Affairs Branch of Army Air Force headquarters in Washington, D.C., in response to an official query about the missing men. The reply was brisk and to the point and barely masked the writer's impatience with military bureaucracy:

Dear Sir:

I received your letter of February 28th and the enclosed form and I feel certain in some way you have been misinformed.

On October 13, 1944, my crew and I bombed Blechammer South, in Germany. We were slightly damaged, but managed to retain formation until we reached Komaron, in Hungary. At that time, due to some error, the formation flew over the Flak area in that locality. We lost a No. 2 engine and our fuel transfer system was damaged.

We left formation and flew on three engines until we were approximately 30 miles northeast of Zagreb, Yugoslavia. At that time we lost another engine and commenced to lose altitude fast. I gave the order to bail out and followed my crew. All ten chutes opened and, although we were machine-gunned from the ground, we all landed safely, with the exception of my engineer, who fractured his ankle.

Second Lieutenant Marvin Tanenbaum, O-687554,

Sergeant Stanley Phillips, and Sergeant John Harlin were captured by the Yugoslavian fascists and then sent to prison of war camps in Germany.

The original report was that all three of these men had been executed. However, by January, 1945, word had been received through the Red Cross that Tanenbaum and Harlin were prisoners of war. No word was heard in relation to Phillips until some time later, since he had been sent to a hospital in Budapest.

All of these men are home and to the best of my knowledge have already been discharged. I fail to see why any additional information is required in relation to any one of them. I take it for granted that this is just another Army "snafu", but if I am wrong, I will be glad to give you any additional information I can.

I remain,

Sincerely yours,

Homer Lane

First Lieutenant, Air Corps, O-822027

The letter was typed on Lane's business stationery; the masthead read "Counselor at Law" and gave his address as One Wall Street, New York City. Assuming Lane remained alive, I wondered if he might still be practicing law. I checked the current edition of a national attorney's directory in the reference room of the Princeton library but found no listing for him. But the library also kept archival copies of the directory, which revealed that as late as 1972, a Homer Lane had worked in the general counsel's office of Mobil Oil, in New York.

When I telephoned an acquaintance who worked in the New York offices of Mobil, he volunteered to find out what he could. The next day, he called back with information that Homer Lane had retired from the firm in 1984. The personnel office had a current address for him in Greenwich, Connecticut, and a phone number. When I called, his wife answered.

"Just a minute," she said. "Homer, it's for you!"

Like Marty Kornbluh and the *Liberty Belle* crewmen I had managed to locate, he was surprised—dumbfounded is probably not too strong a word—to be hearing from me. He vaguely recalled my dad and wanted to know more about my research.

"Well I'll be damned!" He spoke in a gruff courtroom voice that matched my preconceptions; one of my dad's crew remembered his as "a big, heavy-set guy who could talk a blue streak."

I promised to send him some materials, and we agreed to get together for an interview.

It was some months later that I made it to his home in Greenwich. The Lanes were living in a condominium complex with a security guard at the gate, where I stopped to call them. Martha Lane, a pleasant, white-haired woman, greeted me at the curb and showed me in.

Her husband was waiting for me at the top of the stairs— a tall, big-framed man, ruddy faced and with a white crewcut, leaning on a cane.

"Sorry I wasn't down there to meet you," he said, as I climbed the stairs. "They diagnosed me for diabetes a few years ago, and it's harder for me to get around now."

Homer Lane's strong handshake belied his infirmity.

"I recognize you, all right," he said. "You look just like your dad!"

"Except that I'm twenty years older than he was when you knew him!"

On the dining room table he had spread some mementos of Yugoslavia, including a Croatian currency note illegibly scrawled with the names and addresses of several Partisans and a tattered page of notebook paper with the names of the towns they had passed through. We began our conversation at the table, before moving into a sitting room with a large, framed drawing of a B-24. One of Homer's sons, a Navy F-111 radar intercept officer, had given him the picture. Another son, I learned, was an Air Force major on the verge of retirement. In all, the Lanes had four grown children and fifteen grandchildren, with a sixteenth on the way.

While Homer Lane settled into an easy chair, I sat down on the sofa beneath the drawing of the Liberator. Martha was busy in the next room for most of the conversation but stayed within earshot. Every so often she laughed at some comment by her husband and sang out, "I've heard that story a million times!"

Lane had graduated from Columbia University in 1940 and had earned a law degree from Fordham University before he was called to active duty, in January 1943. By the time he completed flight training and shipped overseas, in August 1944, he and Martha were married and the parents of an infant son.

He and his crew flew separately on their first few sorties but were reunited for the mission of October 13 against the oil refineries at Bleckhammer. They were hit moments after bombs away, a burst of flak ripping through the right wing and shearing off the top turret, although somehow the gunner escaped injury—"not even a bloody nose," Lane recalled.

The plane suffered more flak damage en route home. Lane was unable to transfer gasoline between tanks due to a shredded fuel line. Trailing fuel and flying on three engines,

they were losing speed and altitude. The rest of the forma-
tion had left them well behind by the time they crossed into
Yugoslavia and approached Sisak, a city southeast of
Zagreb with heavy antiaircraft defenses.

By now the bomber had dropped to fourteen thousand
feet. "There was no way I was going to fly a lame B-24 into
all those flak batteries," said Lane. "We didn't have enough
fuel left to go around Sisak, and I didn't want to risk a
forced landing. So I ordered everyone to bail out. The flight
engineer let me know when everyone was out. Then he
went, and I put the plane on autopilot, climbed out onto the
catwalk, and jumped."

Descending from fourteen thousand feet, the ten parachutes were sitting ducks for ground gunners, who blasted
away with machine-gun and cannon fire. "All I could think
about was getting hit in the testicles. I went down all the
way holding onto my crotch," said Lane.

He landed in a clearing, removed his chute and stashed it
in the adjacent woods, then ran until he came to a farmhouse. Lane weighed 240 pounds at the time and must have
cut a formidable figure. At any rate, a woman in the yard
took one look at this blond bear in his strange garb and
rushed inside. He ducked into the barn and crawled behind
a pile of hay. It was about half past noon. An hour later, the
farmer returned, heard the story from his terrified wife, and
came out to investigate. As the farmer entered the barn,
Lane stepped out from behind the hay and put up his hands.

"Ingleski!" the farmer exclaimed. "Ingleski!"

Evidently, he thought Lane was an Englishman.

"Americanski!" said the airman, correcting him.

"Ingleski!"

It irked Lane—an Irish-American—to be mistaken for a

Brit. He showed the farmer his dog tags, which had the letters "US" stamped on them.

Satisfied that his visitor, whatever his nationality, was
friendly, the farmer motioned him back behind the hay. Lane
remained in the barn until dark. From a crack in the siding
he could see down the road into the valley. Soon after the
farmer left, he watched, not fifty yards away, a trio of
German soldiers approach, hauling a small field cannon on
what looked like a set of bicycle wheels. They fired several
rounds in the general direction of where Lane and his crew
had fallen—evidently just to scare them, since no one was in
sight. Inexplicably, the Germans made no effort to interro-
gate the farmer and his wife or to search the premises.

That night, the farmer led Lane to the village of Gojilo.
There he found his crew waiting for him, minus the three
missing men. The next morning they marched to Garesnica,
a Partisan town five miles to the north. The crew spread out
on the floor of a farmhouse (the same one Spellacy's crew
had slept in the night before). Lane and his navigator were
quick to accept the farmer's invitation to sleep in his bed,
but they regretted the decision after awaking in the middle
of the night, crawling with lice.

Martha Lane gave me her recollections of those days.
After Homer shipped overseas, she and their infant son
moved into her parents' Manhattan apartment. She tried to
stay optimistic about his chances, even after receiving the
missing-in-action telegram. An undated, vaguely worded
cablegram, sent by Homer shortly after his arrival in Italy,
came at about the same time, leaving enough uncertainty
about his situation for her to assume that he might have
returned safely to base. It was a hope she had to abandon on
receipt of the standard confirmation letter from General

Twining. When she saw a front-page photograph in *The New York Times* of an American bomber being hit over Germany, she couldn't help wondering if the plane was Homer's. At home with her parents for Thanksgiving, she plucked the turkey with tears rolling down her face.

Some of her optimism returned a few weeks later, when a letter from a squadron mate of Homer's hinted that he was now back in Italy. For security reasons, the letter didn't mention Homer by name or go into specifics, so all she could do was read between the lines. She still had not heard from him directly or received any official word of his return. Several days before Christmas, a telegram arrived stating that he was safe but giving no other information. Martha assumed that her husband was in Italy; unbeknownst to her, he was at that very moment aboard a troop ship approaching New York. "It was the night of December 23," she recalled. "Our son, Charlie, had gotten some shots that day and was shrieking and carrying on. I was upset and exhausted when I went to bed and was angry when the doorbell woke me up at two in the morning. I thought it was my sister coming home late, but when I flung open the door, there was Homer."

"With me dufflebag on me shoulder!" Lane said with a grin.

"When I was diagnosed for diabetes a few years ago," he added, "the doctor asked if I was easily depressed. I told him no, that since 1944 I feel like I've been living on borrowed time."

■

Following our visit with Dragutin Vukovic in Casma, we

stopped briefly at the local veterans hall. There was only one person in the small, spare office with the ubiquitous portrait of Tito. Janez merely wanted to check in and get instructions for finding the old Partisan airfield near Miklous, which we wanted to visit. The man—a functionary whose name I wrote phonetically in my notebook as "Konavic"—agreed to take us there.

We drove out of town, through fields of corn trimmed by roadside vines of ripening pumpkin. The airfield site was a broad, fallow plain fringed by forested hills dotted with red tile roofs. Ragweed and Queen Anne's lace nodded in the late afternoon breeze, beneath cruising swallows and a deepening sky cut by vapor trails. According to our guide, this was the principal airfield supplying the Tenth Partisan Corps. American, British, and the occasional Russian plane landed here routinely, often carrying out wounded Partisans to Allied hospitals in Italy.

The featureless terrain evoked no memories on my father's part. Or perhaps he had just repressed them, for the field was a scene of regular disappointment to the airmen, who came out here from Miklous in the vain hope of seeing an American plane. Early during their stay in Miklous, the British secret-service officer informed the crews that two B-25 light bombers were on call at Bari with orders to fly in and evacuate them. But the muddy field and relentless rains made a mockery of these plans.

Just off the road stood a monument to the airfield—a concrete slab supporting a squat, single-engine fighter plane of a type I had never seen. It looked vaguely like an overweight German Folke-Wulf 190.

"Ah, very nice," said Janez, the vintage airplane buff, who circled around it, snapping pictures. He identified it as a Mark 522, a plane of Yugoslavian manufacture and the workhorse of Tito's postwar air force. "This thing really must have been a piece of junk," my dad whispered to me. At Edi's insistence, he climbed onto the slab and posed next to the plane for photographs.

We drove back into town. I was interested in locating the British mission, and our guide took us to several houses where it might, or might not, have been. Nobody seemed to know. Janez translated: "He says that the mission moved many times, that it was some days here, some days there."

It was a similar story when we tried to find any of the houses where the *Liberty Belle* crewmen had stayed while in Miklous. In our vain quest, we parked for nearly half an hour by a house whose owner, we were told, might remember where the crews were billeted. Edi engaged him in an animated conversation, but Janez soon lost interest and drifted off, as bored as Dad and I. I passed the time observing a parliament of fowls in the side yard. A turkey eyed me suspiciously, then went into a strut, fanning his tail in a threat posture. A rooster mounted a hen. A platoon of hissing geese menaced our car as we pulled out of the driveway to return to town. Edi shook his head; even his enthusiasm was waning. In my notebook I scribbled, "All of us getting very tired of all this by now."

It was the end of our third long day of interviews, and the strain was beginning to creep into our routine. Both Dad and I were exhausted, the information was starting to become repetitive, and the farther we ranged from Koprivnica, the less people remembered things specific to the *Liberty Belle* crew.

We had also underestimated the importance of our visits

to local veterans officials, and by now we had had more than our fill of welcoming toasts. Edi and Janez felt it was important to make another courtesy call at the veterans hall. They went inside to see who was there, but Dad and I begged off and remained in the car. "Let's not get stuck here," Dad insisted. It was almost six o'clock. We were due back in Zagreb, and he was worried that the hotel might not hold our reservations.

I wanted to be going, too, but I didn't want to appear rude or do anything to embarrass Edi and Janez. "Maybe we can use our hotel reservation as an excuse," I suggested.

Janez reappeared with the president and other officers of the veterans chapter and leaned into the car window. "They've invited us in for just a few minutes for some *rakija* and beer."

I was wondering what to say when Dad sprang forward in the back seat. "God damn it, Jim—just tell him we've got to get back to Zagreb!"

"Alright, take it easy!" He was right, of course. I turned to Janez. "Tell them we have to return to Zagreb or lose our hotel reservations. They'll just have to understand."

In fact, when we were at last at the hotel it had appeared only about half full, and I couldn't believe we would have such a problem. It would also have been simple to call ahead to keep our rooms. But at this point we all wanted to get back. Janez seized on the excuse and translated it. The old Partisans looked crestfallen, but the president managed a weak grin; still, he didn't give up without a protest. Dad cursed in the back seat, and I could almost sense his blood pressure rising.

I started the car.

"Get in," I told Janez. "We're going."

He jumped into the passenger seat, and I began pulling away before he had even shut the door. The officials hopped out of the way.

"*Velika hvala*! Thank you very much!" I shouted. "*Do vidjenja*—Good-bye!"

Chapter 6
GARESNICA TO GLINA

During the two weeks the airmen spent at Miklous, it continued to rain on and off. The airfield remained a sea of mud that mocked any lingering hope of evacuation by plane. The Partisans spoke vaguely of a better runway—with a hard surface and even lights—somewhere to the south, a few days' walk from here. A Partisan division was heading in that direction (its ultimate destination being Tito's headquarters, in Bosnia), and it was decided that the airmen would accompany it. Late in the afternoon of October 22, a fortnight after the *Liberty Belle* went down, they began moving south and west, in the general direction of the coast.

Soon after they set out, it started raining again. Their march became one of unremitting misery. The rain came down hard, turning the road into a quagmire. Soaked to the bone, cursing, slipping in the mud, they trudged on through the black night, staying together by keeping single file, one man's hand on the shoulder of the next. "Our little march starts," Kornbluh scrawled in his diary, "and before 4 hours are up I'm positive Sherman was right." Meaning, of course, that war is hell.

Sometime after midnight they staggered into the village

of Popovac. The airmen were divided between two billets. Half collapsed on the floor of a house where the Partisans were guarding some Ustashi prisoners taken in an attack on the town of Bjelovar a week before. The others slept in a room with some Partisan women, but "we were too tired to give them any trouble," Rudolph noted. The next morning, they awoke to find a flock of chickens scratching and pecking among them, raising the possibility of eggs for breakfast. Instead, they had corn meal mixed with pig lard, an unappetizing but nourishing pemmican that fueled them for the march to Srp. Selise, a village they reached toward the end of the day. Here they were detached to another Partisan brigade whose interpreter was one Milena Matic, a woman of Croatian parentage born and raised on Long Island. Like the railroad man who befriended Spellacy, she had returned to Yugoslavia for a visit and had become trapped there after hostilities broke out. She was married to a Partisan fighting in another part of the country.

Five miles beyond Srp. Selise was the railroad connecting Zagreb and Belgrade. Guarding it were Cossacks, or "Cherkesi," as the Partisans called them. These legendary soldiers were natives of the Ukraine and for centuries had served as Czarist shock troops. During the Russian Revolution they had fought the Bolsheviks and, twenty-three years later, had embraced the invading Germans as liberators. Some twenty-one thousand Cossacks fought for the Axis in Yugoslavia, mainly in mounted units. After the war, British troops would intern them for a while, then hand them over to the Russians in accord with an agreement reached at Yalta among Churchill, Roosevelt, and Stalin. Most were executed or wound up in Siberian prison camps.

While the airmen waited in Srp. Selise, the Partisans

attacked the Cossack unit guarding the railroad. With the sound of mortars and machine guns coming from the next valley, many villagers found the fighting too close for comfort and beat it up into the surrounding hills. The airmen were assured that the engagement would remain confined to the area to the west, but they stood ready to move out just in case. Rudolph for one was content to stay put, for the Partisans had slaughtered a cow that morning and presented them now with steaks, which they soon had broiling in an outdoor oven. Gorging on the meat, they watched seven Yugoslav-piloted Spitfires roar low over the village to pound the enemy with cannon fire.

The fight ended in a draw, but it stirred up the Cossacks enough that the Partisans thought it prudent to wait a while before attempting to cross the railroad. That evening, the airmen moved to the more secure village of Garesnica, eight miles to the east, where they spent an uneventful week. For food one day the Partisans commandeered another cow. The airmen stood by as they bludgeoned the beast with a sledgehammer, hoisted it from the rafters of a barn, and with a deft slice of a bayonet spilled its guts on the floor. The airmen were ordered to jump on the carcass to help drain the blood. Hunger banished any lingering squeamishness the Americans might have felt as the meat was cut up, roasted, and devoured on the spot. A few days later, they feasted on boiled piglets, eaten with the bristles still on the skin.

While in Garesnica, Spellacy's crew made friends with a Russian physician named Nicholas Birko. A native of Rostow, he had escaped from a German prison camp and was working his way across the Balkans in a roundabout attempt to return home. The doctor was puzzled about the upcoming U.S. presidential election, only a week away. "I don't understand why you bother if you already have a good leader," he said to Marty Kornbluh. "In Russia, if a leader is no good we just shoot him." Birko assumed that Roosevelt would win the election and wanted to know what part of Europe he would seize for the United States after the war.

■

Late in the afternoon of Sunday, October 29, the airmen left Garesnica, moving southwest in a forced march. They re-entered Srp. Selise at dusk, and following a brief rest continued on for about five miles through the drizzly night. Trudging along near the rear of the column, Keith Martin thought he could hear in the distance an approaching train. As the sound grew more distinct, he alerted the Partisans in sign language, opening his palms as if to ask, "What's happening?"

The Partisans threw up their hands, mimicking an explosion. "Boom! Boom!" they laughed.

Meanwhile, toward the head of the column, word was passed to stop and stay quiet. The Partisans planned to blow up the train as it went over a trestle, creating a diversion that would distract the Cossacks long enough for everyone to make a pell-mell dash across the tracks. Huffing its way up the valley, the train seemed to take forever. The airmen were hidden in the woods, on a rise a hundred yards from the tracks, which lay atop a steep embankment. Between them and the tracks loomed a flat, open stretch they would have to cross. They could hear the cloppity-clop of horses' hooves as the Cossacks patrolled the tracks and, louder now, the rumble of the approaching train.

Kornbluh was wearing a raincoat given to him by a girl

in Garesnica in exchange for his fleece-lined flight boots. Sitting in the drizzle on the cold wet ground, he thought of the girl as he pulled the collar of the coat up around his neck.

The train came into view, and as it chugged across the trestle, an explosion rent the night, followed by the screeching of metal and hissing of steam. The locomotive lifted off the tracks and slid partway down the embankment. The Partisans cheered. Some of them opened up with machine guns. Other raced down the hill and across the open area as the Cossacks returned the fire.

The airmen followed after the sprinting Partisans. Kornbluh tripped on his raincoat and fell flat on his face, but he picked himself up and resumed his mad dash toward the tracks. Tracer bullets cut through the darkness. The crack of small arms and machine-gun fire filled the valley, but incredibly no one was hit. Their lungs exploded as they scaled the embankment and scrambled down the other side. Run!

They reached the safety of the woods, but there would be no resting as they continued through most of the night, crossing several streams and arriving at last at another village, where they climbed exhausted into a hayloft. They slept for less than an hour before the Partisans roused them. Milena Matic, their Long Island–born interpreter, told them Ustashi were approaching and they had to move fast. Cursing and groaning, they groped for their shoes and were off on another dash through the dark countryside while the Partisans covered their escape with mortars and machine-gun fire.

An hour or so later, they reached another village and bedded down in another hayloft. They fell instantly into a dreamless sleep.

The next morning the airmen awoke to more rain. They

were now in the broad valley of the Sava River, a flat, marshy region cut by canals. "Whenever we came to a canal," Keith Martin recalled, "we'd wade across it if it wasn't too deep. Otherwise, we had to walk two or three miles down to the closest bridge to cross, and then walk all the way back on the other side. Once, we came to a canal that wasn't too wide. We were going to hike down to the nearest bridge like we usually did, but Carl Rudolph said he was tired of walking and was going to jump it. If he had been an Olympic athlete he might have had a chance. We tried to talk him out of it, but nothing doing, he was so stubborn. Rudy got way back and ran as hard as he could, leaped, hit the opposite bank with both feet, and fell back into the water. We just stood there laughing. He was sitting in water up to his chest. When we saw that the canal wasn't so deep, we waded across."

The valley of the Sava was the scene of another major episode in their hegira. The column had just come through the forest and was sloshing through a field ankle-deep in water. The lowering clouds were only a hundred feet overhead. They heard a dull droning, and a boxy Junker Tri-motor broke through the overcast—the pilot and crew apparently as surprised to see the straggling Partisans as the Partisans were to see them. The German plane banked to the right and moved in for a strafing run. The gunner in the waist door opened up with a machine gun, and as the bullets hit the ground they made little splashes. The Partisans returned the fire, while Merritt took pot-shots at the lumbering plane with his Beretta, to no apparent effect.

Martin recalled the incident later. "I was riding in a cart which didn't have any springs, just the axle connected directly to the body. I sat there bumping along, half asleep, like I was hypnotized. It was morning, and we'd just come through an opening in the forest when this plane came by and started shooting at us. I was too tired to move. The bullets were spraying all around us, but none of them were really close. A few guys were shooting back, but in a half-hearted way. When the plane came back for another pass I finally got out of the cart and hid behind a tree."

Duty done, the Junker flew on its way. Although no one had even been wounded, the incident convinced Martin Kornbluh that he needed a weapon (he had earlier surrendered his service automatic to the Partisans), and in the next town he traded a watch his father had given him for a Beretta.

The strafing was still fresh in Kornbluh's mind several days later, when they came on another group of Partisans guarding three German prisoners in flight suits. One of them seemed just a boy, about Marty's age. Kornbluh was conversant in German and spoke directly to the prisoners. He was surprised to learn that the youngest of them was the pilot of the very plane that had harassed them. The Partisans had succeeded in shooting it down. Like two kids, they exchanged souvenirs—U.S. Army Air Forces wings for Luftwaffe wings. The boy pilot managed a weak smile, then burst into tears. The Partisans were not likely to keep prisoners, and Marty felt pity for the young German who had tried to kill him just a few days before.

The hazards of the road, real and imagined, took their toll on at least one member of the group. A gunner in Spellacy's crew threw a fit one night as they were sitting around a fire. When he began spitting at his fellow crewmen, they wrestled him to the ground and held him down until the crying and kicking stopped. "After that he slept a lot and kept to himself in a corner most of the time," Kornbluh remembered. He would spend most of the next twenty years in and out of the psychiatric wards of veterans hospitals.

They reached the Sava at about noon and crossed it on a barge, landing in the village of Strmen and resting there the remainder of the day. Their hopes about sleeping through the night were dashed when the Partisans moved out again at dusk, hiking along a canal. It was along this part of the route that Art Johnson came down with the flu. Half delirious with fever, he was placed on a horse, his feet tied beneath its belly. Whenever his hunched form began to slip, someone would give a shout and a comrade would prop him up again.

After crossing two more railroads (there were no Cossacks to interfere), they reached the village of Svinjica. Rudolph estimated that the actual distance traveled since leaving Garesnica had been about thirty-five or forty miles, although the rain and mud made it seem like hundreds.

The Partisans told them they would have only a few hours to rest. Making the most of it, they crowded into a cottage, stripped off their wet clothes, and fell dead asleep on the floor. Before noon they were up again and back on the road.

Just before dark they reached another weary village of stucco-and-thatch cottages. This was Prevrsac, where they spent the next five days. Ustashi were operating in the region between there and Glina, twenty-five miles to the west. Glina was their immediate destination, but the Partisans were in no hurry to proceed.

Other groups joined them during their wait in Prevrsac, among them Eastern European refugees and former Allied prisoners of war who had escaped from POW camps in northern Italy. The latter group included Free French, South Africans, Rhodesians, Australians, and New Zealanders captured three years earlier in North Africa and Crete. The Aussie and New Zealand troops spoke bitterly of the British, who they claimed saved their own units in the evacuation of Crete while leaving Commonwealth soldiers to their fate. Many of the South Africans were Dutch-descended Afrikaners whom Keith Martin would remember as "the toughest bunch I've ever seen—big, burly, red-headed guys who would as soon kill you as look at you. They were okay to talk to when sober, but get them drinking and they really turned mean."

Late in the afternoon of the fifth day, Milena Matic announced they would be moving out again. On to Glina and the airfield! But they got no farther than the outskirts of Prevrsac before stopping for the night and bedding down in yet another hayloft. By now—early November—it was dark by six o'clock, and as they had no light they were soon fast asleep.

Several hours later they were awakened by strange sounds coming from the floor of the barn. They could hear slapping, groans, and singing. When Rudolph and Maes peeped through a slat in the loft, they saw five men tied together, seated on a table pushed against the wall. Their legs were bound and extended, and their shoes and socks had been removed, exposing their bare feet. A dozen Partisans and villagers stood to one side, each with a bat-board or broom handle. One of the guards barked an order, and the prisoners commenced another refrain of their doleful song. Periodically the singing was interrupted by the villagers taking turns slapping the prisoners on the feet.

The torture continued through the night. Corbo watched

for a while before trying vainly to get back to sleep, covering his ears to block out the nightmare singing, moaning, and screaming. The next morning, the airmen were told that the prisoners were Ustashi who had killed women and children. Recalling the incident later, Kornbluh remembered the Partisans telling them that they had raped a woman, then cut off her breasts and poured salt into the wounds. Whatever the specifics of the crime, the Partisans were exacting fair punishment as they saw it. By now the prisoners were barely conscious, their feet beat raw and bloody. Their strained voices croaked out a last chorus before they were dragged into the yard and shot.

■

The torture and execution witnessed by the crewmen was just one of many such incidents in a grim cycle of atrocity and reprisal that had marked this region of Yugoslavia on the border between southern Croatia and Bosnia. More than three years earlier, in August 1941, the Ustashi had begun their purge of ethnic Serbs not far from here, in the market town of Glina, where they had herded one hundred and sixty peasants, shopkeepers, and local officials into a Serbian Orthodox church and stabbed them to death with knives.

Glina was the next stop on the airmen's route. Later in the morning of the torture and execution of the prisoners, they climbed into wagons and trundled on their way. Despite the drenching rain of the last few weeks, the road was in fair shape, and they covered the approximately twenty miles between Prevrsac and Glina in less than a day. Once on the road, they began to feel better. The weather had cleared, and the blue sky and rusty hills helped them forget the grim scenario they had witnessed. The understanding that they were headed for a serviceable airfield further lifted their spirits. After a brief stop in Glina—the largest town they had yet seen, with substantial stone houses of two and three stories—they continued on foot toward the airfield. A Partisan told them that transport planes were waiting there to return them to Italy! Marching along, they broke into song. The news seemed too good to be true, and so it proved to be. The airstrip was a demoralizing expanse of mud and water. No plane awaited them, nor could any possibly land there without a week, at least, of dry weather.

Their hopes shattered again, the airmen hiked several miles to a farmhouse on the outskirts of Topusko, a village that in prewar times had enjoyed a certain cachet as a spa. Its mineral baths were still more or less operational, despite a raid by German bombers on the village several weeks before. The attack had destroyed some buildings and killed a few residents but otherwise did no serious damage. Since Topusko had no strategic importance, the reason for the attack was probably the presence, in the farmhouse where the crewmen stopped, of the British mission to the Croatian Partisans. Even this might not have been enough to provoke the Germans but for the man heading the mission: Major Randolph Churchill, son of the British prime minister and a powerful symbol to the Partisans of British solidarity with their cause.

The thirty-three-year-old Churchill and the mission's three other British officers were living in the tiny farmhouse under less than the happiest conditions. Randy Churchill had a gigantic ego and was contentious, garrulous, belligerent, arrogant, and prone to drunken rages. On the positive side, Brigadier Fitzroy Maclean, the British officer with overall responsibilities for Yugoslavia, praised the younger Churchill for his physical courage and noted the "explosive, Balkan, side to his nature," which he believed endeared him to the Partisans.

(Although they often quarreled, the bond between Churchill *père et fils* was strong. In a wartime meeting, Tito noticed tears well up in Winston's eyes when he spoke of Randolph, and before his son's departure for Croatia, the Prime Minister had warned him, "Do take care not to be captured. The Gestapo would only try to blackmail me by sending me your fingers one by one—a situation I would have to bear with fortitude.")

The second-in-command at the Topusko mission was the novelist Evelyn Waugh. Eight year's Churchill's senior, he was dour, sulky, desperately homesick for England, and subject to prolonged fits of depression. A devoutly Catholic intellectual, Waugh had been sent to Croatia with the vaguely defined purpose of wooing Croatian church leaders away from their support of the Ustashi. Although fiercely anti-Communist, Waugh expressed grudging admiration for the Partisans, whose chief characteristics, he wrote, were "youth, ignorance, hardiness, pride in the immediate past, comradeship, sobriety, [and] chastity." They were also "cheerful and respectful, always singing and joking. After the sulkiness of British troops it is extraordinary to see the zeal they put into fatigues." (Waugh's most famous novel, *Brideshead Revisited*, was pending publication at the time of the airmen's arrival in Topusko. None of the airmen in Merritt's group were aware of his literary status, nor did any recall him later.)

Waugh and Churchill came from similar social backgrounds and were old friends. Waugh spoke of Randolph as "preposterous and lovable" and had dedicated his last published novel, *Put Out More Flags*, to him. Both men enjoyed a joke about Tito's sexuality. In their inscrutable private code, he was always "Auntie T" and referred to in the feminine, the Yugoslav leader's robust masculinity notwithstanding. The joke arose out of Tito's shadowy persona during the early years of the Partisan movement, when rumors variously pegged him as a Ukrainian Jew, a Russian general, an American communist, and a woman. (In fact, he was a Croatian and a locksmith by trade.) Word of the joke got back to Tito, and when he met Waugh for the first time, at a beach on the island of Vis, he wore a tight-fitting bathing suit that left no doubt as to his sex. When Maclean, acting as translator, introduced the two men, Tito said, "Ask Captain Waugh why he thinks I am a woman."

The close quarters, constant rain, and Randolph's overbearing personality and incessant drinking, belching, and farting strained to the breaking point the relations between Churchill and Waugh. By the time Merritt's group showed up, in early November, they were barely on speaking terms. Neither man had anything remotely to do of importance to the tactical or strategic situation in the Balkans, and in posting them to Croatia, the British command had relegated them to the most backwater post it could find. During one span, Churchill did nothing but read the Bible on a wager by Waugh and the mission's other officers that he couldn't complete the task in two weeks. The bet was a ruse to shut him up, but it backfired. With a cigar in one hand and a glass of *rakija* in the other, Churchill insisted on reading aloud, complete with such running commentary as, "God, isn't God a shit!"

The mission spent an increasing amount of time caring for the refugees, POWs, and downed airmen pouring into the Glina-Topusko area. As early as the middle of October, Waugh noted in his diary that U.S. air crews were "coming through our hands in large numbers now," and Merritt's group increased to more than seventy the total airmen who had to be housed and fed. It was not a task the British approached with any enthusiasm, and Keith Martin would remember the supreme indifference they met at the mission. "We went into this cottage and found an officer [Waugh?] sitting at a desk. He didn't glance up but just kept writing and ignoring us, like some disgusted clerk in a post office."

■

The airmen were quartered in and around Glina. Spellacy's crew bunked in a partially burned, one-room farmhouse they shared with an older woman, her daughter, and son-in-law. The woman impressed them with her dexterity by picking up live coals in her bare hand and tossing them back into the stove. Early in their stay, they borrowed a tub from the woman and set it up outside. They filled the tub with water and under it built a roaring fire. As soon as the water came to a boil, they stripped to the buff and tossed in their rank clothes. "It took a while to dry the clothes," Spellacy recalled, "and they never looked quite the same again, but we did get rid of the lice."

Lane and his men had been separated from the crews of Spellacy and Merritt since leaving Miklous, and they had arrived in Glina at least four days before them. They were billeted with part of another crew that had been there even longer. Lane remembered spending "hours at a stretch in our bunks, reading whatever we could get our hands on. Any piece of reading material we found would be torn to pieces in half a day as we passed it around, page by page."

The *Liberty Belle* crew was assigned to a two-room farmhouse five miles south of town, in the care of an old farmer and his wife. Their hosts' name was Jednoc. In addition to their two pre-adolescent sons, the Jednocs cared for an orphaned boy whose parents had died in the war—killed by the Ustashi, they said. Rudolph remembered Mrs. Jednoc as "capable, shrewd, and energetic" and her husband as "a typical farmer," tall, with leathery hands and face and a flowing handlebar moustache. The airmen slept in the larger of the two rooms while the Jednocs occupied the kitchen. Mrs. Jednoc's menu of soup and black bread was leavened occasionally by apple strudel made with precious sugar dropped by parachute along with other supplies, courtesy of the Fifteenth Air Force. The Jednocs spoke some German, enough for Rudolph to converse with them. Mrs. Jednoc possessed a country person's intuition about the weather and was free in her predictions. A meteorologist by training, Rudolph often disagreed. As Merritt recalled, "The old lady would come in every morning, wake us up and give the weather forecast. Rudy would give his own, but nine times out of ten, it seemed, she'd be right."

Mrs. Jednoc never missed when it came to predicting snow. "Snega, snega," she pronounced, holding her hands to the sky. It snowed several times during their two-week stay in Glina, although the weather never got cold enough to freeze the airfield, and the only pilot brave enough to land was a woman in the Russian air force. Robert Wheeler remembered her touching down in a C-47, then taxiing back and forth to avoid getting stuck in the mud. "A jeep drove alongside the plane and unloaded supplies. You can forget an American pilot doing that, but she did it all the time." Once, she picked up a Russian liaison officer who jumped from the jeep into the plane. Wheeler recalled that the Russian "spoke some English, and when he said good-bye it was something to the effect, 'I'll see you in the next war between our two countries.'"

The *Liberty Belle* crewmen passed much of the time playing cards, often with the orphaned boy who lived with the Jednocs. To break the monotony they hiked into town, where they found a bustling local economy and their American money greatly in demand. Twenty cents bought a dozen eggs, a quarter a string of roasted chestnuts, a dollar a roasted chicken. A Jewish refugee was a veritable walking jewelry store, with rows of watches for sale, stitched into the lining of his overcoat. Liberated from a concentration camp, he had taken the watches off dead soldiers while working his way across the Balkans, en route to Palestine.

The town boasted a single, tiny theater, and one night it screened a movie that had arrived in the last air drop—"a typical propaganda picture," Keith Martin remembered, "with Robert Young passing as an American worker who refused to give the enemy information about the equipment he was working on, even after they beat him." The movie, made in 1942, was titled *Joe Smith, American*. When the British contingent showed up, Randolph Churchill took a bow. In his diary, Evelyn Waugh complained of suffering through the "revolting American patriotic film."

Except for diarrhea, the airmen were in reasonably good health, although Johnson remained weak from flu, and Merritt had an infected hand, the result of cutting it on barbed wire during one of their night marches. At first, the wound was barely more than a nick, and he had given it little thought, until in Glina it began throbbing in pain and swelled to the size of a baseball. Thoughts of gangrene and amputation loomed in his mind. The British sent him to a Partisan hospital hidden in the Petrovagora Forest, five miles west of Topusko. The Czech doctor who lanced and cleaned the wound had been trained in Prague and possessed exceptional skills, but like the hospital's other physicians he worked without benefit of anesthesia, and screaming rent the wards. Rudolph remembered Merritt returning, after a week's recuperation, in good shape and in a better frame of mind. "While at the hospital, he told me, he became friendly with one of the nurses, but failed to take advantage of the situation even when she mentioned meeting him at night in some abandoned building."

The wretched weather drowned any fantasies about flying out of Glina. As more vagabond airmen and POWs drifted into the area, Churchill on short notice decided to send everyone seventy miles south to the town of Ubdina, which reportedly had a semi-dry airfield. On the afternoon of November 19, the *Liberty Belle* airmen bid goodbye to Mrs. Jednoc. Her husband was working in the fields but came running when he saw them leaving. He pumped each man's hand and kissed every one on both cheeks. Rudolph would always remember the moment of parting and the old man who embraced them so heartily, with the "big smile on his face and genuine tears in his eyes."

With Randy Churchill in the lead truck (a captured Mercedes), sixty airmen and POWs left in a convoy later that day. They spent the night in Velika Kladusa, a village twenty miles west of Topusko, whose mosque and Moslem population reflected the centuries of Ottoman influence in the

Balkans. The next morning they proceeded to Ubdina, but to no one's surprise its airfield turned out to be in no better shape than any other they had seen. Churchill grunted in disgust. After conferring with the Partisans, he decided to send most of the group the rest of the way over the mountains to the coast. The enemy-held port of Zadar (or Zara, as it appeared on the maps supplied in the airmen's escape kits) had just been brought under siege and ought to be liberated in a few days. From there, they could escape by boat to Italy.

The remainder of their trip proved harrowing in the extreme. They were deep in the rugged mountains of southwestern Croatia, at an elevation of forty-five hundred feet, and the road was frozen and dusted with snow. The many switchbacks would have made driving hazardous under the best of circumstances, even without the snow and washouts and the hell-bent zeal of the Partisan driver. Apparently, no one had told him that the truck came equipped with brakes. At every hairpin turn he leaned on the horn. Wehrmacht units were still operating in the area, and the airmen in the back of the open truck were sure he was alerting every German within fifty miles. Merritt would remember this part of their journey as the one time he truly feared for his life. Maes reflected on "that cold, dark and wild ride in the back of the truck going over the mountains" and the Partisan guard, riding with them, whose nose was nearly severed by a wire sagging across the road. The wire knocked him to the deck and blood spurted everywhere, but he was instantly back on his feet. He rode the rest of the way with one hand straddling his gun and the other holding a rag to his lacerated face.

Martin remembered the sheer cliffs and the heart-stopping drop-offs at every turn: "At one place the road had been partially bombed out and was only about half its normal width. We all piled out while the driver tried to get the truck past. It was just like in the movies—he had double wheels in the back, and the outer wheel was hanging over this drop." The driver inched the truck forward, looking back at the wheels with the door open and ready to leap. "He finally got it over. We all cheered, and he jumped out and held up his arms in triumph."

The convoy cut through a pass in the coastal range and dropped down into the valley of the Zrmanja River. Nestled in a bend was the town of Obravac, where they spent several days waiting for the Partisans to complete the liberation of Zadar.

The *Liberty Belle* airmen entered the port Wednesday night, November 22, and were quartered aboard the HMS *Columbia*, a former British cruiser converted to an antiaircraft ship. They welcomed the hot tea and chocolate and the first shower (hot or cold) in nearly seven weeks. Merritt acquired an instant, if temporary, taste for the Irish whisky proffered by the ship's officers, who apologized about being out of scotch. Forever after, he could never understand why the mere whiff of the stuff made him grimace.

The next day—Thanksgiving—the *Liberty Belle* crewmen crossed the Adriatic on a British torpedo boat to Ancona. Following standard procedure, they were ordered immediately to the delousing shack, where they stripped off their clothes and an enlisted man pumping a bellows dusted them with Lysol powder. The treatment "burned like hell," Wheeler remembered, but it killed the bugs. Outfitted in fresh clothes, they boarded a C-47 transport for the short flight to Fifteenth Air Force headquarters in Bari.

Spellacy's crew crossed the Adriatic the same day as Merritt's, but on a different boat. By the luck of the draw, Lane's crew stayed in Zadar an additional four days, pending the availability of another boat. They groused, but the delay was made more palatable by the Thanksgiving dinner of rare roast beef served to them aboard the *Columbia*. Only after their return to Bari did they realize the significance of the delay, which put them beyond the forty-two days in enemy territory needed to qualify for rotating home. Spellacy and his crew had gone down on the same unlucky Friday, October 13, but by returning to Italy on November 23 they came up a day short of the magic number. They were ordered back to flying duty to complete at least thirty-one more missions. Risking a court-martial, one of the men exploded in anger and ripped into the colonel who gave them the bad news.

Like the rest of his men, Spellacy was in a state of shock. He had been looking forward to getting home in time for the birth of his first child, in January. While in Yugoslavia, he had attempted to communicate with his wife by mental telepathy; however effective this might have been, he appeared to her in a dream every night he was missing. Now he could only grit his teeth and make the best of the situation. "I was certain I was going to survive," he would write years later. "I had a wife and a child on the way and plans for lots more, and I was absolutely sure that God would not let all my great plans go to waste."

■

Like the interiors of the other veterans halls we had seen, the one in Glina was sparsely utilitarian, with an old wooden desk and a table, around which eight of us—myself, Dad, Edi, Janez, and four members of the local veterans organization—sat beneath the stern gazes of Marx, Engels, Lenin, and Tito. The room's only other decorative element was a map of Yugoslavia tracing Tito's wartime movements. Although it was only ten-thirty in the morning, the head veteran, whose name I neglected to record but whom I shall call Ivan, had broken out a bottle of brandy for toasting our visit. We had again hoped to avoid such protocols and again had failed.

"Long live the times when we were together fighting in the cause of liberty!" exclaimed Ivan, hoisting his glass. He was a small, wiry man, in a dark suit, white shirt, and thin white tie, with slicked-back hair whose darkness made him look younger than his sixty years. In the fall of 1944, he had been just seventeen, and he could remember escorting a group of airmen between the Sava River and Glina. Mainly he recalled how tired the Americans were, and that one of them (perhaps it was Art Johnson) carried a walking cane.

Ivan proudly informed us that he was president of both the veterans union and the socialist union and also worked in the culture ministry as a reporter. He did not act like any newsman I have ever known, however, and while claiming to be covering our visit, he was doing so without benefit of a notepad or pencil. In one respect, at least, he was the archetypal journalist. The war stories poured as freely as the brandy, and by the time we headed out for a tour of the Glina-Topusko environs, he was oiled to the gills.

Our plans were flexible. I was interested in locating the British mission, but as in Miklous, we were told that it had "moved around" and that no one was sure in what houses it had been. Surprisingly, there was somewhat greater certainty about the quarters for the *Liberty Belle* crewmen. Although Jednoc was a common name in this region, our hosts believed they had located the cottage in which the crew had stayed during its two weeks in Glina.

"We will go there," said Ivan. "Then you will be our guests for lunch."

"Oh, Jesus," Dad groaned. "Tell them thank you, but we really can't."

It was true that we were flying home the next morning and needed to return to Zagreb to pack. By now, we had accomplished just about everything we had set out to do, and in a shorter period than expected, allowing us to move up our departure plans by several days. I had originally thought of tracing my father's travels all the way to Zadar, but we had discovered that the farther we moved from Koprivnica, the more general people's recollections became. We were also tired, and the strain of our trip was beginning to wear on us both. We were a little homesick and missed our wives. The night before, Dad in his typically short-tempered way had been beside himself with frustration over the hotel operator's ineptness at putting through a call to my mother. (Terrorists that day had hijacked a Pan Am plane in Pakistan, and he worried that she might somehow get the idea that we were aboard.)

"We appreciate everything they have planned for us," I told Janez, "but we may not be able to stay the whole day. They have to understand that we must return to Zagreb." Janez translated my concern, but I was not at all confident it registered with Ivan.

The Jednoc homestead was a few miles outside of town, down a dirt road. We parked in the shade of a linden tree and were met by Slanko Jednoc, a pleasant man in a white short-sleeved shirt and gray slacks. A second cousin to the Jednocs who had housed the *Liberty Belle* crewmen, he had been living nearby at the time of their stay. In 1944, he told us, Mr. Jednoc would have been about sixty years old and his wife forty-two, an age difference that fit with Carl Rudolph's account.

There were three cottages in the Jednoc compound, we learned, and all had been occupied by airmen. Two of them were still standing, including the one we were visiting now, which had probably served as the quarters of the *Liberty Belle* crew. It was a handsome old structure of one and a half stories, of a sort that must be common throughout the rural reaches of Eastern Europe, with a steeply pitched tile roof and weathered siding trimmed in a diamond pattern. Slanko recalled that, late in November 1944, a group of airmen lived here for two or three weeks, and that they played a lot of cards.

Stooping through the low doorway, we stepped into the cool interior. Sunlight filtered through the curtained windows of the main room, which was bare except for two rickety beds in the corners. The cottage had been well maintained, but no one had occupied it for several years, Slanko told us.

"Nothing has changed here since the war," Janez observed, and so it appeared except for the portable television we found in the smaller room.

"I remember the TV set," Dad joked. Nodding, he looked around. Although there was nothing specific to jog his memory, the place had the right feel. "This may well be it," he said.

We dropped off Slanko Jednoc at his modern house on the outskirts of town. Finding the cottage where the *Liberty*

Belle crew had been billeted exceeded my hopes for the trip to Glina, and there was nothing more I cared to do but return to Zagreb. Our hosts had other plans, however. Following Ivan's car, we climbed a steep winding road and—surprise!—pulled into the parking lot of a hilltop restaurant.

I was resigned to this, but Dad was steaming about having to endure yet one more of these occasions.

"Damn it, I thought we told him we had to get back to Zagreb!"

"There's nothing we can do about it!" I replied. He was in the back seat, but I do not turn around. Confrontation is not something I handle well, least of all with my father, and I was more upset than I ought to be.

While Dad and Edi followed the others into the restaurant, I lingered in the parking lot with Janez.

"I'm sorry about this, Janez. My father has many virtues, but patience isn't one of them."

"But I can tell—you and your father have a relationship that is special."

It was the last thing I would have expected to hear.

"We do?"

"You are father and son, but you are also friends. You are very fortunate."

"That's nice of you to say."

The lunch took longer than we wished, of course. Ivan sat at the head of the table, chain-smoking and talking a streak. In my notebook I scribbled, "D [Dad] sits next to head of Glina vets org., who goes on and on. . . . D does *not* like him." When Janez bothered to translate, we learned that, like many others in this part of Croatia, Ivan was an ethnic Serb whose ancestors had moved to the region centuries ago. He mentioned the Ustashi massacre of Serbs in the Glina church, adding several hundred to the documented number of victims. Despite his heritage, he lamented the current efforts of Serbian Americans to erect a statue in Washington, D.C., to the Chetnic leader, Mihailovic, whom he regarded as "the greatest tragedy that ever befell the Serbian nation."

We were almost finished with dessert when he asked my father to describe again his Vienna mission and the bailout over Koprivnica. After listening to the story, he turned to me.

"And you were living at the time?"

"I was six months old."

He grinned and turned to Dad.

"You see then, you are younger than your son! For when you jumped out of the plane, you were born again."

Chapter 7
GOODBYE, *LIBERTY BELLE*

In the weeks before our departure for Yugoslavia I had felt a growing sense of unease. In part I worried about acquiring the materials I would need for writing a book. As far as I knew, our guides, Selhaus and Zerovc, had not planned a specific itinerary, and I could only hope that they had done sufficient advance work to make our trip a success. When I mentioned this concern to a friend, an author who travels widely to write about people he has never met, he tried to reassure me. "You have every reason to feel the way you do," he said. "No matter how much preparation you put into something like this, you can never be sure about these things until they work out. I think you'll get what you're looking for, but you're *right* to be worried—I can completely understand it."

But my apprehension went deeper. I was uncomfortable as the initiator and organizer of our trip, a reversal of the usual father-son roles. And I still had trouble gauging my father's enthusiasm: Did he really want to go through with this, or was he doing it because *I* wanted it? Eventually I came to realize that his interest had less to do with reliving his past than it did with sharing the experience with me.

From the start of the project, I had noticed a reticence on his part. Only later did I interpret this not as a lack of enthusiasm but as an avoidance of pushing too hard. We did a lot of dancing around each other's feelings.

When I told a female colleague about my trip, she was empathetic. "My mother and I went to Vienna together for a week last year. We got along fine, and the companionship was important to both of us. But unless your relationship is really unusual, inevitably there's going to be some tension. It's not like traveling with your sister, say, or a friend. You tell yourself you're an adult and ought to be able to deal with it, but the parent-child thing makes it a lot harder. You want everything to go perfectly, even when you know that it won't."

We would be leaving from JFK International Airport the evening of Labor Day. Too soon, it seemed, the weekend arrived. The closer Monday loomed, the more hare-brained the venture seemed.

"I can't believe I've gotten myself into this!" I said to my wife, Nancy. "What if everything goes wrong?"

"You and your father are going to have a wonderful time," she said. "Think how lucky you are to be doing this with him."

I didn't feel lucky at all. Monday came, and in a few more hours Nancy would be driving me to my parents' house to begin the first leg of our trip—a limousine to Newark Airport, and from there a helicopter ride to JFK. I had butterflies in my stomach. It seemed I was departing on a long journey, although in fact we expected to be away only a week. It was a perfect morning; a front had moved through during the night, and there was a snap of fall in the air. An hour before we left, I drove out to the retail orchard where our daughter Jennifer was working. I found her among the apple trees in the pick-your-own section of the orchard, a big blond kid two weeks short of seventeen, cheerfully directing customers. I thought of our trip the previous March to California to interview *Liberty Belle* crewmen and of how far I had come in my quest during the five months since. In a couple of days, she would be heading off for her third and final year at boarding school. It had been nice having her home, but soon she would be leaving us again.

"Oh Daddy, have a great time with Poppy in Yugoslavia," she said.

"I'll be up to school in October to see you. Can't wait."

Saying goodbye to my daughter recalled another parting. It was almost twenty years ago to the day, I realized, that I had gone off to Navy Officer Candidate School.

I had left for OCS on a Saturday morning, with plans to spend the night in New York City before taking the train the next morning to the naval base at Newport, Rhode Island. It took me only a few minutes to pack, as the civilian clothes I would be needing over the next four months fit easily into an overnight bag. Looking around my bedroom—at the books I had grown up with, the stack of old phonograph records, the dusty model airplanes I had labored over as a twelve-year-old—I felt no particular nostalgia. For the last seven years, between boarding school and college and summer jobs as a camp counselor, I had become a transient in my parents' house. Parting was the most casual thing in the world.

I had mixed feeling about going into the service, but it was not all dread. Perhaps the heady freedom I'd enjoyed during my last three weeks in Europe, hitchhiking through

Italy and France, made it easier to accept the absence of freedom I would soon be experiencing. I said good-bye to my mother and grandmother, promising, if possible, to come home on a weekend leave later in the fall. My father drove me to the bus stop in Upper Montclair. The route took us along Upper Mountain Avenue, a residential boulevard lined with baronial mansions set back on rolling lawns. We made conversation for a bit but were mostly silent as we drove along the maple-lined way. I sensed that my life was changing, although just how much I could not imagine. Over the next ten months I would receive my commission, become engaged, fly halfway around the world to meet my ship off Vietnam, and marry on a whirlwind leave following my ship's return to its home port in Hawaii. It did not occur to me to wonder what might be going through my father's mind.

We parked at the bus stop and waited in the car, across from the Bellevue Theatre, where I remembered as a kid my mother taking me to see *Snow White*. There was little to say, and I was relieved when the bus appeared around the corner and pulled up in a rush of air brakes. The doors swung open, and as people began boarding I got out of the car and in line. Dad stood with the overnight bag and handed it to me as I got ready to board. We shook hands, rather formally. Then he clapped me on the shoulder and squeezed.

"So long, Jimbo."

"I'll see you soon," I replied.

I climbed quickly into the bus and grabbed a seat, putting the overnight bag in the place next to me so that I would have both seats for myself. I didn't look back, and as the bus pulled out I stared dumbly at the neat suburban plaza. The bus accelerated, and the familiar shops and streets slipped by.

Suddenly I was crying. It burst on me without warning, as suddenly and unexpectedly as a summer storm. Not just a few tears blinked back but a paroxysm, a torrent that overwhelmed me with its swiftness and power. I was bawling, sobbing uncontrollably. The rush of emotion and my inability to control it astonished me. I was confused and more than a little embarrassed.

The bus moved onto the highway now and was speeding through the vast ugliness of the Hackensack Meadows toward New York City. I sat back in the seat and took a deep breath. In the calm that settled over me I began to understand. I had left home for good.

■

Similar emotions washed over me as I lay in the hotel room in Zagreb during our first night in Yugoslavia, wondering again what it was that I was trying to accomplish. But my anxiety and confusion gave way to confidence and a renewed sense of purpose once Edi Selhaus and Janez Zerovc arrived the next morning and we proceeded through the bright fall countryside to Koprivnica.

Two days later, on Friday, September 5, we are ascending a gravel road toward the crash site of the *Liberty Belle*. It was several miles outside of Koprivnica in what showed on a local map that Janez had given me as the Vincegora Forest.

The four of us were driving in one car, following in the dusty wake of another. It was eleven o'clock, and we had already packed a full day's activity into the morning, including our meeting with former Partisan Adreja Celescek and a stop at the farm where Dad and his crew had assembled after the crash. The platoon of journalists and cameramen that had followed us for the last two days had blessedly shrunk to a reporter and photographer from the Koprivnica paper, *Glas Podravina*, and its indefatigably cheerful editor, Dragan Desnica. A beaming, round-faced man in his early fifties, he had taken an acute interest in our story. His English was even more limited than my Serbo-Croatian, but he had managed to teach me the expression for "nice day," and at each of our several stops this morning we gestured toward the deep blue sky and exchanged a hearty "*Lep dan!*"

Dragan was in the lead car with his reporter and photographer and our guide to the crash site, a local farmer named Branko Herak. A rugged, stocky man with angular Slavic features, Herak was in his late fifties. We learned that he had six grown children, including three sons who were also farmers, and six grandchildren. His wife worked in Berlin and sent home five hundred marks a month, surely the lion's share of their income.

Gravel gave way to dirt, and soon the road was scarcely more than a gash cut through the oak and beach forest. We passed a logging site with heavy equipment parked next to stacks of felled and trimmed tree trunks. Herak told us that he had been fifteen years old at the time of the *Liberty Belle*'s crash and had guided Partisans through these woods. As such, he felt deserving of a veteran's pension and was bitter that the government had denied him one on grounds that he had never officially been part of any Partisan unit.

Our cars strained up the last steep stretch of road and came to a stop at the end. Engines cut, doors slammed, and we were immersed in the silence of the woods. From the clearing where we parked, we hiked another fifty yards through ferns and grass to the top of a ridge. Herak pointed into a ravine that fell away on the other side. It was here, he told us confidently, that the *Liberty Belle* had met her flaming, spectacular end. "I was in the village when the plane came over. I saw it circle and ran up here with the others when we heard the crash."

The villagers had stripped the Liberator carcass as thoroughly as piranhas. The last part of the plane to be salvaged, Herak recalled, was a tire that survived for some years after the war. Although nothing now remained, it was apparent that the woods here had been cleared sometime in the past. The surrounding forest was much denser, with trees reaching upwards to sixty feet, while those in the ravine were perhaps half that height. Looking up at the older trees, Dad marveled at their size. "You can see how a parachute could get caught here."

While Dad and the others remained on the ridge, I followed Janez into the ravine. Although the chances were remote, I was hoping to find some small, overlooked part of the plane—I would have been satisfied with nothing more than a rusty bolt. Midway down, I stopped to rest and looked back at the others who had remained behind. The noonday sun filtered through the trees, warming my back. A breeze came up, and Dad's voice drifted toward me, mingling with the rustling of leaves. He was talking to Edi, describing, yet again, the last moments of the *Liberty Belle*. From my vantage I tried to imagine the scene forty-two years before—the screaming bomber ripping through the forest, the fiery explosion, and the parachutes floating toward the trees.

Janez, meanwhile, continued to search, his eyes glued to the ground, criss-crossing back and forth with the single-mindedness of a bloodhound seeking a scent. I was back on the ridge now with Edi, who told me in his halting English, "Janez is optimist. We work ten years in these projects—always he finds things." But today it was not to be.

The lack of physical evidence notwithstanding, the spot *looked* right and jibed with the testimony I had collected. Dad, for one, was satisfied that we had found the site of the *Liberty Belle*'s crash. "My memory of this part is clear," he said. "This is pretty much what I expected to find."

Later, Selhaus would send me his account of these events, casting them in a different perspective. Standing next to my father, wrote Edi,

> I watch him and believe that I know what he is thinking;
> yes, more than forty years ago he experienced real luck:
> first that he did not die in the plane, and secondly that he
> had landed among the Partisans. . . . I do not know if he
> believes in God, but I think he is saying prayers at this
> moment, giving thanks for the good luck with which his
> life has been endowed. His son, who is with him today,
> was only six months old at the time; and he is here to write
> his father's story.

Edi claimed to see tears in my father's eyes. Maybe so. Neither Dad nor I is sentimental by nature, but for both of us, this was the climax of our trip. As my pain and doubt melted away, I realized our fortune at sharing this experience. Perhaps Dad was indeed thinking along the lines suggested by Edi. How could he have imagined, on that sultry afternoon in October 1944, that, under such different circumstances, he would one day stand again in this forest in Croatia?

Before leaving, I tried to explain to Edi the pun behind the name "Liberty Belle." Somehow, I succeeded—helped by his fluency in Italian, whose word for pretty is "bella," and the fact that he seemed to know of the Liberty Bell in Philadelphia, whose picture I crudely rendered in my notebook.

Comprehending the play on words, Edi smiled. "Here is the last place for this beautiful dama."

Looking into the ravine, Dad nodded. "May she rest in peace," he said.

NOTES

See the bibliography for complete names of sources.

Chapter 1

- The description of the base at San Giovanni and the routine there (pp. 8–14) comes mainly from the author's interviews.
- The description of the pre-mission briefing derives from the same sources, from Fifteenth Air Force Mission Summaries, and from Ardrey; Anderson; Birdsall; Muirhead; and Bailey, *The Air War in Europe*.
- Status of Luftwaffe planes and pilots (p. 11–12): Morrison, p. 267.
- Effectiveness of German antiaircraft batteries: Bailey, *The Air War*, pp. 118, 137–38, and Overy, pp. 121, 144.
- The importance of oil depots and refineries as targets, and the rivalry between the Eighth and Fifteenth Air Forces: Birdsall, *Log of the Liberators*, pp. 218, 229.
- Flight equipment (pp. 18–19): interviews; Birdsall, *Log of the Liberators*, p. 240; Bailey, *The Air War*, p. 98; Ardery, p. 136.
- Number of sorties for passage home (p. 13, 20): interviews.
- Median age of airmen (p. 21): calculated from dates of birth on Missing Air Crew Reports.

- Tail markings and construction details of the *Liberty Belle* (p. 22): *Fifteenth Air Force Story*, p. 52; Birdsall, *Log of the Liberators*, p. 313.
- Liberator versus Flying Fortress: interviews; Liberator Club *Briefing*, Winter 1972, p. 2.
- Number of B-24s built: Birdsall, *B-24 Liberator*, p. 309.
- Cost of Liberator: Sheehan, p. 82.
- Preflight and takeoff procedures (pp. 23–26): interviews, *Flight Manual for B-24 Liberator*, pp. 27–28.
- Combat formation (p. 26): Bailey, *The Air War*, p. 89; interviews.
- Number of planes turning back, route to target (pp. 32): Mission Summaries.
- Discomforts of flying (p. 32–33): Bailey, *The Air War*, p. 88; interviews.
- Casualties (p. 37): Missing Air Crew Reports.
- Norden bombsight (p. 37): Bailey, *The Air War*, p. 88.
- Accounts of being hit and bailing out (pp. 38–40) are based on personal interviews and correspondence, not all of which exactly correlates. Johnson, for example, recalls that Wheeler, not Carver, was the first one out of the back of the plane, while Martin believes he jumped first (but he was in the front of the plane and would not necessarily have known what was happening in the back). See also Johnson's account in Ambrose, pp. 161–63 (which errs in stating that this was Merritt's first mission).

Chapter 2

- Accounts of rescue by Partisans (pp. 41–51): personal interviews.
- Details about Ivan Serbec and the other Yugoslavs who helped in the rescue come from correspondence with Edi Selhaus, who found and interviewed Serbec at his home in Zagreb.
- Loss rates during Big Week and on the Ploesti raid of August 1,

1943 (pp. 65–66): Morrison, *Fortress without a Roof*, pp. 134, 200.

Chapter 3

- The bombed village (p. 77–78): The identification of the village as Topolovac is based on Carl Rudolph's account. Topolovac is about ten miles south of Vrhovac, where the *Liberty Belle* crew spent the first night. In both his manuscript, "The Walk Back," and in his annotated map, Rudolph indicates that the crew spent all of October 8 in Topolovac. It is possible, however, that the bombed village (which both he and Art Johnson describe in their reminiscences) was actually Poganac. Located about a mile west of Vrhovac, Poganac was the regional Partisan headquarters. When interviewed in September 1986, several surviving Partisans suggested that the crew held up for the day in Poganac.

  The author has stuck with Topolovac as the probable village for several reasons. Rudolph's account was written within several months of the crew's return, so would be closer to the actual events than the recollections of people forty-two years later. Also, the crew, after rousing in the middle of the night of October 7–8, traveled several hours (perhaps as many as six), before reaching the bombed village, so must have covered a distance closer to ten miles than one mile.

  In 1990, former *Liberty Belle* crewman Art Johnson and his wife, Polly, visited the crash site at Vrhovac and also went to Ludbreg, the site of the Partisan congress that Johnson and Cunningham had attended on October 8, 1944. In a letter to me, Johnson wrote that, at the time of his visit, the owner of the farm buildings in which the crewmen had spent their first night told him he would be tearing down the old structures the following week. On the Johnsons' visit to Ludbreg, they were accompanied by Tomo Blazic, the photographer who had taken pictures on that day forty-six years before. There, they met

Dusanka Skoric, age eighty-two, who had been present at the congress and remembered Johnson's speech. Art reported that the courtyard and buildings where the congress had been held had changed little.

Prior to going to Yugoslavia, the Johnsons had been in Vienna, where they visited the island in the Danube that had once been the site of the Winterhaven Oil Works. Most of the island has remained undeveloped since the petroleum facilities were destroyed in the raid of October 7, 1944.

• Political and military situation in Yugoslavia preceding and during World War II (pp. 79–80): Bailey, *Partisans and Guerrillas*, pp. 71–89; Clissold, *Whirlwind*, pp. 98–102, 132–133, 150–53, 164–69, 215–19; Brajovic-Djuro, *Yugoslavia in the Second World War*, pp. 208–9, 220; Cochran, "Time Out for Conquest."

Chapter 5

• The black airmen (pp. 149–51): The author confirmed the identity of the two black pilots after publication of the first edition of *Goodbye, Liberty Belle*. The accounts of Chandler and Westbrook are based on interviews with them and another Tuskegee airman, William A. Campbell, in 1995. See also Francis, *The Tuskegee Airmen*, which mentions Chandler and Westbrook as well as two other 332nd pilots who wound up on the ground in Yugoslavia. On October 12, 1944, according to Francis, lieutenants Luther "Preacher" Smith of Des Moines, Iowa, and William W. "Chubby" Green of Staunton, Virginia, while returning from an escort mission strafed a railroad junction on Lake Balaton in Hungary. They hit a barn filled with high explosives that blew up, damaging their planes. Smith made it to. the Yugoslav border, bailed out and was captured. Green circled, realized his plane had been hit, too, and bailed out. He was picked up by Partisans and four days later was flown to Naples by a Russian plane. Copies of the missing air crew reports for Green and Smith corroborate this account. Smith's plane was hit in the gas tank. He was wounded in the arm and wound up in a hospital in Zagreb before his transfer to a POW camp.

- Dogs (pp. 152, 158): As both Spellacy and Kornbluh heard dogs barking as they descended in their parachutes, there evidently were a few canines left in Yugoslavia—not all had been eaten, as my father assumed, based on his not having seen any dogs during his forty-nine days in-country.
- "Blechammer" (p. 159): Also spelled "Bleckhammer" and "Blechhammer," this was a site, in a corner of western Poland annexed by the Third Reich, of synthetic-oil refineries.

Chapter 6

- Cossacks (pp. 172–3): Bailey, *Partisans and Guerrillas*, pp. 120–21.
- Ustashi atrocities in Glina (p. 180): Clissold, *Whirlwind*, pp. 93–96.
- Topusko (pp. 181–88): Bailey, *Partisans and Guerillas*, pp. 118, 122; Sykes, *Evelyn Waugh*, pp. 260–69; Roberts, *Randolph*, pp. 266–77; Haller, *The Grand Original*, pp. 83–97; Leslie, *Cousin Randolph*, pp. 88–103; Davie, *The Diaries of Evelyn Waugh*, pp. 568–93.
- Jednocs (pp. 185–87): "Yednoc" was Rudolph's phonetic spelling of the name of the farmer in whose house the crew stayed while in Glina. Maes remembered it being pronounced "Yodnec."

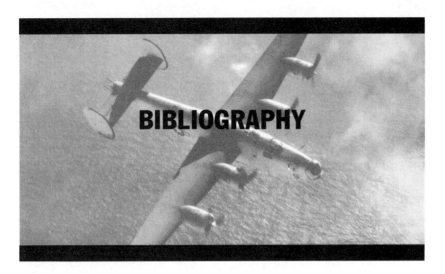

BIBLIOGRAPHY

Manuscript Sources

Unpublished accounts by downed airmen Michael Spellacy, Arthur Johnson, and Carl Rudolph.

Missing Air Crew Reports for Fifteenth Air Force, October 1943–April 1945.

Fifteenth Air Force Mission Summaries for October 7, 1944.

"Escape Statements" of Nicholas Corbo, et al., November 26, 1944; and Martin Kornbluh, November 27, 1944.

Books

Ambrose, Stephen E. *The Wild Blue: The Men and Boys Who Flew the B-24s Over Germany.* New York: Simon & Schuster, 2001.

Amory, Mark, ed. *The Letters of Evelyn Waugh.* New Haven, Conn.: Ticknor & Fields. 1980.

Ardery, Philip. *Bomber Pilot: A Memoir of World War II.* Lexington: University of Kentucky Press, 1978.

Anderson, William C. *Bomber Crew 369.* New York: Bantam, 1986.

Bailey, Ronald H. (and the editors of Time-Life Books). *The Air War in Europe.* Alexandria: Time-Life Books, 1981.

————. *Partisans and Guerrillas*. Alexandria: Time-Life Books, 1978.

Birdsall, Steve. *Log of the Liberators*. Garden City, N.J.: Doubleday, 1973.

————. *The B-24 Liberator*. Famous Aircraft Series. Fallbrook, Calif.: Aero Publishers, 1968.

Bowman, Martin W. *Castles in the Air*. Wellingborough, Eng.: Patrick Stephens, 1968.

Brajovic-Djuro, Petar V. *Yugoslavia in the Second World War*. Belgrade, 1977.

Clissold, Stephen. *Whirlwind: An Account of Marshal Tito's Rise to Power*. London, 1949.

Craven, W. Frank, and James Lee Cate, eds. *The Army Air Forces in World War II*. Chicago: University of Chicago, 1955.

Davie, Michael, ed. *The Diaries of Evelyn Waugh*. Boston: Little, Brown, 1976.

Dedijer, Vladimir. *History of Yugoslavia*. New York, 1974.

Fifteenth Air Force: The First 40 Years, 1943–1983. March Air Force Base: Directorate of Public Affairs, Fifteenth Air Force Headquarters, undated.

Flight Manual for the B-24 Liberator. Appleton: Aviation Publications, 1977.

Francis, Charles E. *The Tuskegee Airmen*. Boston: Bruce Humphries, Inc., 1953.

Halle, Kay. *The Grand Original: Portraits of Randolph Churchill by His Friends*. Boston: Houghton Mifflin, 1971.

Kaplan, Philip, and Rex Alan Smith. *One Last Look*. New York: Abbeville Press, 1983.

Leslie, Anita. *Cousin Randolph*. London: Hutchinson, 1985.

Morrison, Wilbur H. *Fortress Without a Roof*. New York: St. Martin's Press, 1982.

Maclean, Fitzroy. *Eastern Approaches*. New York: Atheneum, 1984.

Muirhead, John. *Those Who Fall*. New York: Random House, 1986.

Overy, R. J. *The Air War, 1939–1945*. New York: Stein & Day, 1982.

Roberts, Brian. *Randolph*. London: H. Hamilton, 1984.

Rose, Robert A. *Lonely Eagles, the Story of America's Black Air Force in World War II*. Los Angeles: Tuskegee Airmen, Inc., 1976.

Rust, Kenn C. *Fifteenth Air Force Story*. Tempe City: Historical Aviation, 1976.

Sherry, Michael S. *The Rise of American Air Power*. New Haven: Yale University Press, 1987.

Sykes, Christopher. *Evelyn Waugh, a Biography*. Boston: Little, Brown, 1975.

Periodicals

Briefing (publication of The Liberator Club, San Diego), #7, Winter 1972; #35, Fall 1986.

Cochran, Alexander S., Jr. "Time Out for Another Conquest." *World War II*, May 1991.

Shaplen, Robert. "Tito's Legacy." *The New Yorker*, March 15 and 22, 1984.

Sheehan, Susan. "A Missing Plane." *The New Yorker*, May 26, 1986.

Interviews

Liberty Belle crewmen: J. I. Merritt, Gil Carver, Nicholas Corbo, Arthur Johnson, Keith Martin, Carl Rudolph, Don Maes.
Others: Homer Lane, Martin Kornbluh.

INDEX

OTHER COOPER SQUARE PRESS
TITLES OF INTEREST

HITLER'S WAR
Edwin P. Hoyt
With a new preface
440 pp., 60 b/w photos, 4 maps
0-8154-1117-0
$18.95

JAPAN'S WAR
The Great Pacific Conflict
Edwin P. Hoyt
With a new preface
568 pp., 57 b/w photos, 6 maps
0-8154-1118-9
$19.95

THE GI'S WAR
American Soldiers in Europe during
World War II
Edwin P. Hoyt
With a new preface
664 pp., 29 b/w photos, 6 maps
0-8154-1031-X
$19.95

WARLORD
Tojo against the World
Edwin P. Hoyt
With a new preface
280 pp., 10 b/w photos
0-8154-1171-5
$17.95

INFERNO
The Fire Bombing of Japan,
March 9–August 15, 1945
Edwin P. Hoyt
170 pp., 10 b/w photos, 2 maps
1-56833-149-5
$24.95 cl.

**THE INVASION BEFORE
NORMANDY**
The Secret Battle of Slapton Sands
Edwin P. Hoyt
212 pp., 22 b/w photos, 4 maps
0-8128-8562-7
$18.95

GUADALCANAL
Edwin P. Hoyt
314 pp., 43 b/w photos, 10 maps,
1 diagram
0-8128-8563-5
$18.95

**TRAGIC FATE OF THE
U.S.S. *INDIANAPOLIS***
Raymond B. Lech
336 pp., 52 b/w photos, 2 maps
0-8154-1120-0
$18.95

Available at bookstores; or call 1-800-462-6420

COOPER SQUARE PRESS
200 Park Avenue South
Suite 1109
New York, NY 10003-1503
www.coopersquarepress.com